SANTERIA

A Practical Guide to Afro-Caribbean Magic

LUIS MANUEL NÚÑEZ

Spring Publications, Inc.
Woodstock, Connecticut

© 1992 by Spring Publications, Inc. All rights reserved
Second printing 1993
Published by Spring Publications, Inc.
P.O. Box 222069; Dallas TX 75222
Printed in the United States of America on acidfree paper
Cover design and production by Margot McLean, using a painting
of a Santeria ceremony by Jsabel dos Santos (private collection)

Library of Congress Cataloging-in-Publication Data
Núñez, Luis Manuel.
Santeria : a practical guide to Afro-Caribbean magic / Luis Manuel
Núñez.
p.   cm.
ISBN 0–88214–349–2 (pb)
1. Santeria (Cult)   I. Title.   II. Title: Afro-Caribbean magic.
BL2532.S3N86   1992
299'.67—dc20   92–24219
                                                        CIP

Contents

CONTENTS

Santeria and the Idea of Sacrifice

MOST OF WHAT'S TAKEN FOR GRANTED IN SANTERIA IS SUCH AN ASSAULT on Western thought that Luis Manuel Núñez has written an intensely provocative book simply by being elegantly clear and descriptive. Take, for instance, the book's last entry, "Where to Obtain the Ingredients [for rituals]":

"If you live in a large city with a pronounced Latin population, you should have no trouble. Look in your Yellow Pages under 'Religious Articles and Supplies.' Any business with a name like 'Elegua's' or 'Botanica' will be able to provide anything you need. Many of the Ebos described in this book are available pre-mixed and packaged, as aerosol sprays and as Ebo "kits.""

"To obtain animals for sacrifices, look in the Yellow Pages under 'Pet Stores.' Look for those stores in the same neighborhood as the 'Botanicas.'"

These paragraphs imply a lot. There are now few large cities in North America *without* "a pronounced Latin population," so the practice of Santeria is going on all around us, such a part of our collective daily fabric that the trusty Yellow Pages are all we need as both proof and guide. In fact, estimates put the number of Santeria worshipers in North and Latin America conservatively at one hundred million. The great Latin American migration to the United States shows no sign of abating, so Santeria will become more and more a part of American life. In cities like New York, which is now more than sixty-five percent non-white (depending on which unreliable census you believe), it's common to find evidence of Santeria and other West African-influenced religions on many streetcorners and in most parks. Crossroads being holy places in these religions, in the gutters of the Bronx you'll see burning candles surrounded with ceremonial cigars and designs, while burnt-out candles amidst little piles of bones have become part of the landscape in places like Brooklyn's Prospect Park.

The practice of Santeria isn't confined to churches because that is the nature of Santeria's gods. While the gods of Judaism and Christianity, according to their scripture, walked among us long ago and promised to come again one day, the gods of Santeria are *here*. They are not archetypes or complexes, as psychology would have it; they are not dead, as existentialism would have it; and, while they can be intoxicating, they are certainly not opium, as the Marxists would claim. They sing, walk, talk, dance, joke, heal, curse, and save, through a process that the West usually classifies as psychotic but which millions in Santeria experience with no evidence of psychosis: possession.

As Núñez describes in detail, the purpose and heart of the Santeria ceremony is to invoke one or several gods and goddesses through ritual and music, especially drumming, so that the *Orisha,* as they are called, will visit and possess some participants in the ceremony. Through these people, the *Orisha* will answer questions, warn, advise, consecrate, or do whatever the god or goddess feels like doing. A god may possess a woman, a goddess may possess a man, without any sexual stigma or innuendo. Gradations and subtleties of sacred states and behavior are enacted not only before your eyes but within your body—or you watch your mother or brother go through it. That's not at all like sitting still while a minister preaches about some far-off divinity or a therapist theorizes about one's anima.

What in the West would be called "inflation" (at best) is an experience common to all in Santeria: the *Orisha* speaks through your very flesh. Which wouldn't be possible if flesh were, by its nature, suspect. (No Cartesian mind–body split around here!) To be in your body is a beautiful thing, and the gods prove it by joining you in your body. Is it surprising that peoples with centuries of such tradition move more easily in their bodies than Judeo-Christians for whom the body is suspect?

Just as there is no mind–body split, in Santeria good and evil are not polar opposites, struggling in the figures of God and the Devil. As with the Greek pantheon (which the *Orishas* strikingly resemble), each god in Santeria is capable of doing good *and* evil. This confers two great benefits that the West lost with monotheism. First, a much more subtle concept of morality: in the wonderful *Orisha*-tales called "apataki" collected here by Luis Manuel Núñez, we see how many-sided *any* behavior is, whether intended as good or bad, and how important it is to differentiate among gradations of behavior. Second, Santeria, like the ancient Greek religion, doesn't need to concentrate all evil into one figure, one Satan, because every god sometimes acts destructively; without a satanic figure, there is far less temptation to project shadow-elements and negativity outside of oneself. One cannot be better than the gods, and if the gods are destructive and irrational at times that doesn't mean they're "evil"; it means that destructive and irrational things happen in life, and they are to be lived with, guarded against, fought, healed, forgiven, understood, and remembered, but not stigmatized as coming from the source of all darkness. Life, in Santeria, is returned to the realm of *event* rather than judged by abstractions.

Another Western truism that Santeria denies is that we live and die essentially alone. From the Catholic confessional to the novels of Sartre and Camus, this is what people assume after two thousand years of the belief that an all-mighty God of the Universe devotes His entire attention to judging *you* as an individual both in life and death and that, no matter how many people come to church, the drama of the ritual is strictly between you and this God (with the priest, minister, or rabbi as kind of a referee). In contrast, Santeria's rituals are communal. Nothing important can take place without drummers and people willing to cook the food, prepare the place, and participate; even if a given ritual is focused on one person, like an initiation, it requires a community to properly meet and honor and give their bodies to the Orishas. Nor are the Orishas solitary entities. The apataki tales in this book illustrate beautifully how the story of one god includes other gods, and, as with people, a god's properties will alter in the presence of others. And then there are the dead to be considered. Every Santeria ritual begins and ends with a blessing for the ancestors, and the dead are accorded almost as much honor and service as the Orishas. It is even said that an enemy who has died may be more powerful and harmful than when alive. Death looms in Santeria not as judgment or oblivion, torment or paradise, but as another kind of life that lives alongside of, and participates with, this one. The dead *remain part of the community.*

If you cannot think of your gods as isolated, you cannot think of yourself as isolated; if even the dead have a place in your community, then certainly you do—no matter who you are or how you've lived or what anyone thinks of you. Over the next decades, as Santeria and other West African-rooted religions become more and more a part of North

American life, it will be fascinating to see how they change the basic assumptions that govern our culture. Especially a Santeria practice we've not discussed yet: animal sacrifice.

Most rituals of Santeria involve some sort of sacrifice—as have most religious rituals throughout history all over the world to this day. Some of Santeria's sacrifices can't help but feel extreme, at least to my Western sensibilities, such as this prescription of a private "ebo" to "escape the law": "Rub your head with two quail hens. Bite their heads off and let the blood drip on your head. Spread their feathers up and down the street." (It's not too hard to understand *that* one: anybody who could hype themselves up to do it is obviously in a prime state of mind to do whatever's necessary to escape the law.) More elaborate ceremonies, like initiations, often involve the sacrifice of many, many birds, goats, and such. And this is where Western sensibilities often part company with Santeria.

But why? It can't be a strictly moral objection. With all our Burger Kings, Colonel Sanders, steaks, and barbecues, American daily life requires an enormous amount of slaughter. Our supermarket shelves are full of it. Whether these creatures are killed for food or for ritual surely is all the same to the creatures. A culture that considers it just fine to throw a live lobster into boiling water and then eat it can't claim any high-ground on Santeria's treatment of animals. America is a long way from going vegetarian; and recent plant research indicating that plants, too, can suffer makes even vegetarianism suspect. (Joseph Campbell defined a vegetarian as "someone who can't hear a tomato scream.") Why, then, do Westerners excuse the killing of a certain class of animals for lunch but not for ritual?

I think our abhorrence has two sources. First, there is our attitude toward ritual—an attitude unconscious and therefore unadmitted, but powerful. European Judeo-Christians are a people who have had their sacred rituals done *for* them for many, many centuries. Our rituals have been officiated by specialists who do nothing else, in places where we do not live. Until comparatively recently, these rituals were even done in languages that most of us couldn't understand. Our insulation from ritual, when compared to other cultures, has been extraordinary. To put it mildly, we've lost the knack. Direct participation in ritual is almost unknown to us except for weddings, bar mitzvahs, and such; and, whatever the celebration may be like afterwards, the actual ceremonies are

fairly subdued and strictly presided over. To do rituals *yourself;* to have
no insulation between you and the sacred; to have to take the responsibility in your own hands, the passion in your own heart, the meta-
physics in your own head; to stand before your own divinity with nothing
between you and eternity but your frail intentions—most Westerners'
engrained terror of such things is expressed reflexively, even compulsively,
as embarrassment, repugnance, fear, and cynicism.

Which brings us to our second source of abhorrence to Santeria's
animal sacrifice, namely, the West's deep confusion about *any* kind,
or level, of sacrifice; its guilt about the entire concept of sacrifice. Santeria
and Voodoo are rooted in the West African Yoruba civilization, and
the scholar Robert Farris Thompson translates a Yoruba word for
"devotee" as "he, she, who extends both palms, gives, sacrifices." We
are nervous enough of "extending both palms," that is, of personally
conducting ritual; but even "to give" has become a suspect act among
us—much less "to sacrifice"! We have lived so long by an economics
in which giving and personal sacrifice are penalized brutally; an
economics which rewards selfishness to a phenomenal degree; an
economics dependent on a kind of institutionalized blindness to anyone
else's needs, or to the needs of the community—we have lived so long
by such an economics that the idea of *any* genre of sacrifice is deeply
threatening. It literally threatens our livelihood, our security, our sense
of how to get things done.

At the same time, the economic rules we live by commit enormous
sacrifices, brutally but impersonally. In the name of individual and cor-
porate profit we sacrifice the very ecology of the planet; we sacrifice
huge segments of the population to poverty; we sacrifice the safety and
health of our cities; and in war we take it for granted that we must
sacrifice innocent non-combatants. So when we see, in a Santeria
ceremony, that some hens or goats are sacrificed, we project into this
act the horror, confusion, and guilt of all the sacrifices our way of life
calls for on one level and all that it forbids on other levels. The animals
themselves are of no consequence: we wouldn't object to eating most
of them. It's the direct, messy contact with ritual and the idea that only
by some sort of sacrifice, some inner or outer offering, can the divine
be invoked; it is the very idea that animal sacrifice is both the symbol
and test of the deeper, inner sacrifice the devotee is prepared to make—
this is what makes Westerners shiver, turn away, and condemn. For it

follows that people who are willing to sacrifice as little as we must be very far from the divine.

"Sacr-ifice" has the same root as "sacred," and our word "bless" comes from the French "wound": these concepts are intimately bound in our psyches, and the practices of Santeria stir them up, challenge them, bring them to consciousness. Which is one of the greatest gifts that Santeria has for the West. As it seeps more and more into North American culture over these next decades, as its ethics and ways inevitably influence us, it can't help but expose how we've gone slack, how we've become hypocritical and dull to what was best in our traditional religions.

This doesn't mean that you and I have to start killing chickens to be devout. But Santeria does remind us that the sacred is, at the very least, a two-way street, and that it is not enough to ask the gods to bless us. We must bless them as well and find a way to bless their world.

MICHAEL VENTURA

DISCLAIMER

THE INFORMATION IN THIS PUBLICATION IS PRESENTED SOLELY FOR ITS ethnographic interest.

Neither the author nor the publisher endorses the practices and procedures described in this publication in any way. Nor do they assume any liability for any use a reader may make of the information, practices, or procedures described in this book.

INTRODUCTION

SANTERIA IS NOT AN ARCHAIC RELIGION. IT IS A VIBRANT FORCE WITH five hundred years of continuous history in the Western Hemisphere. Its African roots go back at least as far as Christianity's.

Santeria has millions of followers spread across the United States, the Caribbean, Central and South America. There is Voodoo in Haiti, Macumba in Brazil, and Candomble in the northern coasts of South America. Its adherents come from all walks of life: doctors, lawyers, politicians, thieves, and pimps. All those who seek the power to control their own lives and want to lead them in accord with the deepest parts of their beings are candidates for initiation into Santeria.

As the traditional belief systems of the Western world cease to provide a direct emotional involvement with the mysteries of life, more and more people are turning to the throbbing of the Santeria drums. It is a religion of trance, mystery, possession, blood, and sex.

What follows is a brief glimpse into Santeria. If you want to know more, go to the ceremonies, burn the candles, and dance to the drums. Neither skin color nor language is a barrier. The ancient gods will recognize their own.

Historical Notes

SANTERIA'S ROOTS ARE IN AFRICA, IN THE YORUBA RELIGIONS NATIVE to Nigeria. It was brought to the New World by the hundreds of thousands of men, women, and children who were hunted down and sold as slaves.

The African religions had to undergo severe transformations in order to survive. The changes that led to Santeria began in 1517, when Yoruba slaves had their first bitter taste of Catholicism in Cuba.

It is its Catholic content which gives Santeria its peculiar flavor. The combination results in a Santero's being a devout Roman Catholic at the same time he or she is sacrificing a rooster to a cement image of Elegua enthroned behind the front door.

There are no records. There are only stories, echoes of voices long dead.

The slave is brought to the new land. No longer a human being, the slave is sold and traded like a beast of burden. If the Master is kind, the slave will eat and live to work. If the Master is not, the slave will work until the slave dies.

Night brings an old Yoruba song. A homemade drum answers. A chorus forms. More drums are brought out. The old movements are recalled. The dancing starts. Chants and dances from quarreling African tribes join and make love to each other. The rhythms unite, transform, and give birth to something new.

The herb man looks after the sick. He sees the future. Prayers. Offerings. Sacrifices. He knows what foods the gods like, what women attract them. Enemies are killed by a handful of powder.

The white man in the black cassock comes. There is a Jesus. He was tortured and killed. His mother cries. The slaves understand grief and death.

The white god doesn't talk. The white god does not come to visit. The white god does not like the things that the earth gives with such love. No singing. No dancing. No food. No perfume. He hates the feel of soft velvety flesh and laughter in the night. The white god makes no miracles.

The old Yoruba priest teaches the young the ancient rites. Secretly. They are treasures.

Nannies croon African Apatakis. White babies fall asleep, the stories of the gods in their ears. The babies grow up. They dance. They believe.

White men have black lovers. Beautiful black women bite their ears. They learn to respect Chango. They do not provoke Elegua.

The Spanish Inquisition comes and kills and burns. They say there is only one god.

The slaves smile and lie. They worship Chango, Obatala, or Oshun as they kneel in church. They believe in the white god and saints as well. The more love and respect given to all the gods, the greater their protection.

Elegua, the playful messenger of the gods, cheerfully becomes the Holy Child of Atocha. Oshosi, the fierce god of war, shrugged his shoulders and became St. Norbert. Oshun, the hip-swinging goddess of those who know how to make love with skill and passion, became Our Lady of Charity (La Caridad del Cobre). Chango, the invincible warrior chief, the whoring god of storm and lightning, showed his sense of humor. He turns into St. Barbara.

Everyone felt much more protected now that Chango was a warrior as well as a female Saint inside the church. No one fooled anyone. The slave owners saw that, after a religious festival (a "golpe de Santo"), there was peace and harmony in the sugar plantations. Many white mothers had their children brought back to health by a black herbalist. Young women swore about the effectiveness of love philters and showed off their handsome husbands as proof. The priests thought about the recent slave uprisings in Haiti and the accompanying massacre of the priesthood and assured the laity that a little drumming in the night was absolutely harmless.

Santeria was born. No one really paid much attention.

CHAPTER TWO

Ceremonies

THE RULE OF OSHA, AS SANTERIA IS FORMALLY KNOWN, HAS NO WRITTEN canon. Its traditions are passed on orally to the initiates. The written records in existence are either direct transcriptions from the oral tradition taken from initiates by interested researchers or from the notebooks in which a godmother or godfather laboriously wrote, with a smeary pencil, awful grammar and spelling, the finer points to be remembered during the ceremonies. The Lucumi language that the initiate in Santeria, the "asentado," is supposed to learn and practice is passed on in the same way.

Santeria has many variations according to the locality in which it is practiced. Distance and necessity make many of the practices vary wildly from each other. However, certain common threads run through all practices and make it possible to come up with what may be called a "generic" ceremony.

The Ceremony

It is Saturday. Everyone arrives early, dressed in their patron Saints', their *Orishas'*, favorite colors and bringing the collars (*Ilekes*) and bundles and boxes containing the sacrificial animals and special foods and offerings needed for the ceremony. The ceremonies are long and exhausting. They can last all night and into Sunday morning.

A large, comfortable room has been reserved in the house. The time passes in conversation, jokes, and anecdotes. The altar is placed in a prominent position within the ceremonial area. Commonly, images of Christ and St. Barbara are prominently featured. Spread out before each image is a large ceramic soup tureen with a cover, usually decorated in a very rococo style. These tureens contain the stones (*Otanes*) sacred

7

to the Orishas and the consecrated cowrie shells (*Dilogun*) used in the shell oracle (*Medilogun*).

Upon the mat covering the floor before the altar, the participants place the fruits, vegetables, cooked foods, and the sacrificial animals they brought to the ceremony. There are also containers of *chequete* (a drink made from sour orange juice, molasses, corn meal, and fresh coconut milk). Bottles of *aguardiente* (an extremely strong drink distilled from sugar cane juice) are also placed on the mat as an offering to the Orishas. The official conducting the ceremony, either a high-ranking bishop (*Babalawo,* or *Iyalocha,* if a woman) or a common priest (*Santero* or *Santera*), will fill his or her mouth with the aguardiente and spray it over the gathering as a blessing and to quiet those who have been possessed by an Orisha during the ceremony.

The conversation dies down at a signal from the Babalawo. Everyone settles down in front of the altar. The Babalawo holds up a container of *Omiero* (a mixture of rain water, river water, sea water, and holy water; aguardiente, honey, corojo butter—extracted from the hard nuts of the corojo palm, cocoa butter, powdered eggshell, pepper, and various other herbs and ingredients peculiar to the mixture's purpose. It is brewed by immersing a live coal wrapped in a fresh taro [*Malanga*] leaf into the mixture, which has been steeping since the previous day).

The container is presented to the four cardinal points, and a small offering is made to each by spilling a bit of the Omiero. The Babalawo faces the altar and offers the Omiero to the Orishas, asking them to bestow their magical powers (*Ashé*) upon him. A little Omiero is then spilled at the room's entrance. The Babalawo returns to the center of the gathering and spills Omiero on the floor three times. The mixture is then offered to whomever would like to drink. Almost everyone does.

The Babalawo then draws the required symbols on the floor to summon the Orishas. They are drawn with powdered eggshell mixed with earth from the roots of the favorite tree or plant of the house's tutelary Orisha. The symbol is blessed and sprinkled with corn meal. A candle is lit at prescribed points. No one walks on these designs or steps over them.

The preliminaries being over, the youngest initiates (young in terms of time since their initiations into Santeria), along with those who aspire to join, back into the room, their faces away from the altar. They make obeisance by lying face down on the floor with their heads toward their godmother or godfather, the person sponsoring the novice and who may or may not be conducting the ceremony. This person or persons, in turn, salute the Orishas and bless the new initiates and the novices. The blessings made, the godfather or godmother stands. The drumming begins.

Sometimes a participant is immediately possessed by an Orisha. At the moment of possession, the personality traits of the controlling Orisha become clearly manifested. Shaking and shuddering of the whole body are followed by very strong convulsions. The possessed individual falls on the floor.

The physical symptoms cease. Utter calm is reflected in the "montado"'s face (literally, he who is ridden; the act of possession). Voice, mannerisms, and gestures change completely. The personality of the "caballo" (horse) ceases to exist. The personality of the Orisha has completely taken over the believer's body.

Nearby persons restore the "caballo"'s calm by blowing into his or her ears and mouth. Cocoa butter or corojo butter is rubbed on the person's hands and feet. If the trance becomes too violent, the "caballo" may be injured. It is the responsibility of those around the possessed individual to ensure his or her well-being.

After the initial crisis is over, the Orisha's control over the possessed body becomes stronger. The Orisha dances to the welcoming beat of his or her specific rhythm and chant and "cleans" (purifies and blesses) those present. If the ceremony includes an animal sacrifice, the Orisha blesses those present by tearing or biting off the heads of sacrificial birds and sprinkling them with the blood.

If the Orisha is in a good mood, his "children" (those initiated to that particular Orisha) will joke and dance with the Saint. If the Orisha is in a bad mood or comes to punish someone, there is a profound silence. Everyone respectfully listens to the scolding.

The Orishas speak briefly and get directly to the point. They prefer to communicate through the cowrie shell oracle or the coconut oracle (*Biague*).

The trance may last for seconds or for the entire ceremony. The trance's end comes spontaneously, although the godmother or godfather of the possessed person may have to intervene at times and prevent the possession from lasting too long a time. This is especially true in the case of a novice whose trance capacity is not well-known. Rarely can the possessed person remember what he or she did or said.

The Initiation (The "Asentado")

The details of each initiation ceremony vary according to the Orisha who will become the "parent" of the person being initiated into Santeria. The following information is a composite obtained from various sources and may be described as a "generic" initiation.

The first Orishas to be "asentados" (literally, seated upon) the novice's head are Obatala, Chango, Yemaya, and Oshun. Petitioning these Orishas for protection, offering them blood sacrifices, and becoming possessed by them mark the entrance of the novice into Santeria.

The novice has no say in selecting the Orisha whose "child" he will become. The relationship is revealed through consulting the oracles, the physical characteristics peculiar to the "children" of a particular Orisha, and through the direct intervention of the Orisha as he or she possesses a person and lays claim to that person prior to his or her novitiate.

> I remember that the first thing I had to do was to get together the money. And it was a lot! An asiento is expensive. The big one is the fee to the Babalawo, but there's also all the food to buy and the aguardiente. Not to mention all the new clothes I had to buy. You have to have all new clothes, you know, to be clean.

Both the money and the new wardrobe are turned over to the novice's godmother or godfather. It is this sponsor who administers the funds.

The current cost of an initiation in New York or in Miami can easily run from three to five thousand dollars. The cost is determined by the Orisha, or so it is said.

> My godfather came and told me when the asiento was going to be. I was very excited. I was frightened, but I was mostly excited. I packed up my things and moved to my Babalawo's house. I was supposed to be there a week, but I had problems at work and I had to go back to work in four days.

If the novice is a girl who has reached the age of menstruation, the date of the "asiento" and of its accompanying rites must not correspond with that of her period. The proximity of a menstruating woman to an Orisha is considered sacrilege.

> The Babalawo sat me down in his room. He made me sit on a mat.
> He took out his shells and sang to them and shook them up. Then,
> he had me blow into them to give them Ashé. He threw them over
> and over again until he was sure what my *Ebo* was going to be.
> I've been pretty bad, so, let me tell you, it was a lot!

An Ebo is any sacrifice or offering to the Orishas. In the case of an initiation, the Ebos are the sacrifices the novice must make to appease the Orishas offended by his or her past faults or evil actions.

> They brought in this big cage full of birds. There was everything
> in there. Chickens, roosters, pigeons, everything. I'm standing there
> in front of everybody, and the birds are making a hell of a lot of
> noise. The Babalawo takes out the birds one by one and rubs them
> all over my body and hair. There was chicken shit everywhere. He
> then took out his knife and killed all the birds. That was scary.
> And I had to taste the blood.

Once the Babalawo has transferred the novice's impurities to the birds, the Orisha's names are called out. Each of the sacrifices is described to the Orishas in Lucumi, an archaic form of a language still commonly spoken on the Nigerian coast. The Babalawo is very careful to explain what is wanted of each Orisha. The novice is then presented to the images. They are begged to accept the novice into Santeria.

> We stayed chanting for a long time. Then, the Babalawo cleaned
> me up a little bit. We all got in cars and they took me to the river.
> We got there just as the sun was setting. It was beautiful.

After making Ebo to the Orishas, the novice must be taken to a place holy to his or her patron Orisha.

> I was crying and glad that Oshun had chosen me. She is my favorite.
> I took the plates of food that we had all prepared for Oshun and

> went down into the water. I put the food in the river. Not like throwing it away, but with respect. When I had given all the food to Oshun, I ripped off my clothes and threw them in the water. That was great. I was naked in the water in front of all these people, crying and feeling really happy.

The novice is then carefully bathed in the river by the Babalawo with the help of the accompanying Santeros and Santeras. The ceremony is very much like a full immersion baptism. The novice is then dried and wrapped in a new towel.

> Then, I filled my new pot with the river water. We all got back into the cars and went back to the house. No, no. I wasn't naked any more. I had on my new clean clothes. When we got back to the house, Eduardo was whaling away at this big cow bell. It was just like church, but happier. Then, I had to take off my clothes again and get washed in the water from the pot.

That night, the Babalawo petitions ("rogar") the novice's head. A person's head is inhabited by an *Eleda,* a guardian angel. The Eleda is not an Orisha. If the Eleda is ignored and proper attention is not given to the resident angel, it will abandon the person, who will become defenseless against evil influences. The intelligence will be lessened. Without feeding a person's Eleda, no important rite can take place. The Eleda is fed by drinking blood.

The Ebo to petition the Eleda is fairly simple. Doves are sacrificed and their blood is tasted by the congregation. Two deep dishes are filled with powdered eggshell, two coconuts, cocoa butter, cotton, cooked but unsalted corn meal, bread, guinea pepper, smoked fish, jutia (a large Caribbean rodent about the size of a possum), and slugs. The Babalawo places a white cloth on the floor before the soup tureens containing the Otanes sacred to the Orishas and places the deep dishes on the cloth. Two candles are lit and placed to either side of the dishes.

A *Moyuba* (prayer of invocation in Lucumi—see page 79) is offered to the Orishas, the spirits of the dead, and the dead Babalawos, Iyalochas, Santeros, and Santeras.

They lit the candles and sat me in this tiny chair right in front of the altar. First, I had to take off my shoes and roll up my pants. Then, I sat on the chair with my hands on my knees.

The Babalawo takes a gourd full of water and spills it on the floor three times. He prays to Olodumare: *"omi tuto, ana tutu, tut laroye, ile tuto olodumare ayuba bo wo ebe elese olodumare ayuba bai ye baye to nu."*

The Babalawo makes Moyuba to the dead Elders and to the spirits of the dead: *"ibaye baye tonu bowo oku be lese olodumare mo yuba ibaye bafayaye kosi iku kosi aron kosi ina dosi eye kosi faya kosi ofo ariku baba wa."* He then makes Moyuba to the Orishas, beginning with Elegua.

The Babalawo picks up the two deep dishes and stands before the novice: *"emi bori* [name of the novice] *kosi iku kosi aro kosi ina kosi eye kosi ofo ariku baba wa."*

My knees are starting to cramp up a little bit by now, all scrunched up in that chair, but the Babalawo is still standing in front of me with the dishes. He says that they have this and they have that. I don't understand very much of it. Anyhow, he touches the dishes to my feet and then to my knees and my hands. He comes a little closer and rubs the dishes on my shoulders and my forehead, and a little bit on my neck. I'm starting to smell a little strange when he smears cocoa butter on my feet. But, he takes most of everything off with big wads of cotton. Then, he took white powder and made lines on my face. I tell you, I felt like an Indian.

The white powder is powdered eggshell. The Babalawo draws three small horizontal lines on the novice's cheeks, forehead, hands, knees, and feet. If the novice is a woman, the lines are drawn vertically.

The Babalawo breaks a coconut and selects four pieces. He then picks out a meat fragment from each piece: *"oni no iku, obi no aro, oni no eye."* With the hand holding the coconut flesh he touches the novice's forehead, neck, shoulders, chest, hands, and knees. With the same hand, he touches the floor and his own forehead: *"ile mo ku ko ori mo ku ko."* The Babalawo throws the small pieces of coconut on the floor three times: *"obi aremi."* He stands behind the novice: *"kekueku."*

> He put the pieces of coconut in his mouth, after throwing them
> on the floor and everything, and he chewed them up with a bite
> of cocoa butter. He spit it out on his hand and put it all over my
> head. I don't know. In my friend's asentado, the *Iyawo* [novice]
> used a blender. That seems better, you know?
>
> Anyhow, then he put the white collar around my neck. So, with
> Obatala with me, I felt better. Stronger.

The placement of the first collar is a crucial moment. It is the time
that the novice's relationship with the Orishas "catches."

> A couple of the women helped me get up, because I was all cramped
> up. They took me outside the room and sat me down on a white
> sheet they had laid out for me. They told me to shut up and stay
> quiet.
>
> I didn't see why, because everyone outside was laughing and talk-
> ing. There were a lot of people there, because you need at least
> sixteen Santeros to do an "asiento."

Osain, the god of herbs and healing, is the next Orisha invoked during
an "asiento." To "make" Osain, herbs must be broken up and ground,
crushed and mixed. This portion of the ceremony is generally entrusted
to a herbalist of proven experience. The herbalist goes out into the
wilderness, or to an empty lot next door, to obtain the *Ewe* (the herbs).

When the herbalist returns, he must announce himself and the herbs
at the door: *"ago ile egbe onareo ago ile."*

> When he got back, he gave these big bundles of herbs to the
> Babalawo. The Iyalochas laid out clean mats on the floor, and
> everyone helped to spread the herbs out. The Babalawo gave them
> water to drink and coconuts to eat. Then, he spit on them. He
> said it was to give them Ashé.

Seven ceramic pots, painted in the symbolic colors of the Orishas
(white, red, blue, yellow, black, green, and brown), are set out among
seven barefooted Iyalochas. The herbs are distributed. Each Iyalocha
receives the herbs belonging to her patron Orisha. Each Iyalocha goes
on to offer a Moyuba to her Orisha as she receives the herbs.

The Babalawo intones the prayers for the dead and the prayer for Olodumare and initiates the sixteen ritual chants, beginning with the one for Elegua (see page 79).

Each Iyalocha prepares her herbs and places them in her pot. The contents of all the pots will go to make the Omiero, the all-purifying water. It regenerates and cures because in it are concentrated the powers of the medicinal plants and the influence of the Orishas.

The Omiero is formulated as follows: the Otanes, the lodestones sacred to the Orishas, are washed with their corresponding herbs. The Orishas' ornaments and their cowrie shells and collars are washed as well and then dried with white linen cloths.

The washing of the lodestones begins with those belonging to Elegua. The stones are steeped in the herbs belonging to him (see the "Herb" sections in chapters four to seven).

Ogun's stones are washed next. Then follow the Otanes of Oshosi, Obatala, Chango, Agayu, Yemaya, Oshun, and Oya.

The sap extracted from the pounded leaves is mixed with rain water, river water, sea water, coconut milk, and holy water, honey, aguardiente, corojo butter, tiny bits of smoked fish, jutia, cocoa butter, powdered eggshell, toasted grains of corn, and guinea pepper. The mixture is poured into a tub, and a small live coal wrapped in a taro (Malanga) leaf is dropped in. The Omiero will tonify the body of the Iyawo (novice) and prepare him or her to receive the presence of the patron Orisha.

> When they finished washing the Orisha's stones, the Babalawo came and threw a white sheet over me. I couldn't see anything. I was stood up and someone walked me to a door.
>
> "Knock," the Babalawo told me. So, I knocked.
>
> "Who are you looking for," he said. "Osain?" I said, "No." "Yemaya?" "No." We went like that, back and forth, until he said, "Oshun?" and I said, "Yes."
>
> Someone opened the door and pushed me through. Something warm and sticky went on my feet, but the Babalawo told me to keep my eyes closed.

After dripping the blood of a young chick on the novice's feet, the Babalawo leads him or her into the room by the hand. The novice is made to kneel in the tub full of Omiero and is washed once more by each of the Santeros present. If the novice is a woman, she is washed by the Iyalochas. He or she is then dried with the towel used after bathing in the river. The novice is then dressed in new white clothes.

> I felt really good and smelled really good too. I sat on a chair, and an Iyalocha put a sheet around my shoulders. The Babalawo started to shave my head, and the Iyalocha made sure that none of the hair fell on the floor. That would have been bad luck. When my head was shaved, the Babalawo started to paint it for the Orisha.

The novice's head must be prepared to ease the Orisha's entrance and possession of the body. First, a central circle, the color of the Orisha who will possess the novice, is painted. Circling it in a bull's eye pattern are seven concentric circles in white, red, blue, yellow, black, green, and brown. Below the circles, all the Babalawos, Iyalochas, Santeros, and Santeras paint dabs of color, each one using the color of his or her patron Orisha.

> After everyone finished painting my head, they sat me on the "pilon" [a large upright mortar] that was used to mash up the herbs. The Babalawo put water in Oshun's herbs and made a mud out of it. Then, he put the mud all over my head.

Each of the Santeros and Santeras participating in the ceremony daubs a little bit of the herbal paste on the novice's head until it is covered in a helmet-shaped plaster.

> The Babalawo started to pass the Otanes to me. It was pretty emotional. This was the first time that I'd been allowed to touch them. The last ones they let me hold belonged to Oshun herself. Between handling the Otanes and the singing for the Orishas and the drums, I started to feel very strange. Things started spinning around me like I was getting drunk. It was like a big hand was squeezing my chest so that I couldn't breathe. I started to shake really hard. I couldn't help it. The singing got louder. The Babalawo started singing right next to my ear. Then, I don't remember anything.

The patron Orisha is being enticed and cajoled to enter the novice's body. When the physical symptoms indicate that the Orisha has taken possession of the body, the Babalawo shouts: *"iya ye kuma kue yu mao!"*

He tears off the head of a guinea hen and touches the bleeding neck to the novice's mouth so that the possessing Orisha can drink the blood. Immediately, tiny pieces of smoked fish, jutia, pepper, a little honey, and a sip of Omiero are given. The Babalawo lightly incises a cross on the novice's tongue with a razor.

The Babalawo opens the possessed novice's eyes and gives his thanks to the Orisha: *"gbogbo koyu mo dupue."* The Orisha has manifested its presence. The "asentado" is effective. All the participants shout and sing. Everyone gets up to dance. The Babalawo and his assistants help the novice return to consciousness and wipe off all the Ashé from his head with a white cloth, in which the sticky remains are wrapped and carefully saved.

CHAPTER THREE

The Sacrifice

Right after they cleaned all the stuff from my head, my Babalawo started to kill the animals. It took hours to kill everything. If I could have afforded it, it would have taken all day. But, who has that kind of money?

ONLY A BABALAWO OR AN IYALOCHA MAY KILL. IF THEIR PATRON Orisha is Ogun, their rights to slaughter need only be confirmed in a brief ceremony. The "children" of other Orishas must have the sacrificial knife granted to them over a period of long and involved rituals and initiations, by a Babalawo or Iyalocha who has Ogun as his or her patron Orisha.

All the animals have to be healthy, beautiful, and fat. I spent days running around making sure that they were perfect.

It's very important that everything be the way the Elders did it when the Orishas are being fed. Because, if the Babalawo doesn't know what he's doing and screws up the sacrifice, the "asentado" won't work. Not only that, you could die, or the people that are there could get sick, or their children could get sick. Blood is very powerful: you can't fool around with it.

You have to feed the Orishas. The blood gives strength to the Orisha and the novice. It made me stronger. People can't do bad "work" against me. I've been baptized in the all powerful blood, the life of life.

The sacrificial killing establishes a strong bond between the novice and the Orishas. The same benefits extend to those that participate in the sacrifices.

The animals are kept outside the *Igbodu* (the room containing the altar and consecrated to the Orishas) until the moment of their sacrifice. Animals with four legs, covered by colored cloths, are brought into the room first. The color of the covering indicates to which Orisha they will be sacrificed. All the birds have their beaks and legs washed with Omiero.

All the tureens, filled with their Otanes, are placed on the floor and left uncovered. The Babalawo makes an offering of water and coconut to each tureen: *"omi tutu laro ero pesi labe koko lodo per leri wi bo mo iga be ri iga boya iga bo chishe ile mo koko mo peloni intori iku mo peloni intori iku aye mo pe loni intori ofo mo da bi pe loni ebsoe iku obi aro obi aye obi ofo obi lebareo."*

> I was feeling a little better, but I had to stay seated on the "pilon" and was told not to move.
>
> Two Iyalochas led in a lamb. The Babalawo gave it some sunflower leaves. She ate them. That was real good because it meant that Oshun liked the lamb.

"Firolo firolo bale fi ro lo ba le abo fi ro lo fi ro lo bale abo fi ro fi ro lo bale."

> The Babalawo gave me some pepper and a piece of coconut meat to chew up. I spit it back out on his hand, and he smeared it on the lamb's head. He brought the lamb close to me, and I had to touch her three times with my forehead and rub my forehead and my balls on her.

If the novice is a woman, she rubs against the animal with her breasts and legs.

The Babalawo's assistants tie the animal's legs together, and it is placed on the floor on a bed of banana, guava, and poplar leaves. The Babalawo takes up the knife: *"yakina yakina."* The helpers respond in chorus as they stretch the animal's neck. Chorus: *"bara yakina yakina yakina lo bara yakina."* The Babalawo stabs the animal in its jugular vein, and the fountain of blood is caught in the Orisha's tureen: *"ogun choro choro."* Chorus: *"eye ba re ka ro."* Babalawo: *"eye ogun moyu re ebima."*

As he kills each animal, the Babalawo shouts, "I did not kill it; Ogun, who is great, killed it," removing all guilt and responsibility for his actions. Chorus: *"ebima eye ogun moyu re ibi ma."* Babalawo: *"elegua dekun."* Chorus: *"eye dekun ye."* Babalawo: *"olodumare eye eye."*

He cuts the lamb's head off. The Babalawo pours salt in its raw neck wound: *"iyo iyo ma le ro iyo iyo ma le ro."* Chorus: *"abala iyo ma le ro abala iyo ma le ro."* The Babalawo smears corojo butter on the bleeding neck stump: *"te epo epo ma le ro te epo epo ma le ro."* Chorus: *"abala epo epo ma le ro abala epo epo ma le ro."* He smears honey on the neck: *"ba ra i la wi oñi o ba ra i la wi oñi."* Chorus: *"odu ma ma la wi oñi o ba ra i la wi oñi."*

> Then, the Babalawo put the head right on my face, and I drank the blood. I looked up at the ceiling and spit all the blood up to the Orisha.

With the head, the Babalawo twirls around the novice and then offers it to the Orishas: *"ato reo ato reo afori mawa orio oba to ba ofori mawa adere mo ni o adere monio fa ra ori lori elewa ode rere monio odere re."* He places the head before the tutelary Orisha's tureen: *"ten ten leri fu mi ba fo wa o ten ten."*

The headless carcass is removed from the Igbodu by the Babalawo's helpers. They hold it up by the legs, making sure that the neck stump faces the door. The Babalawo places a rooster or a coconut between its rear legs: *"wo ekun eni le wo ekun eni le wo ekun eni le."* At the door, the carcass is turned to the left and to the right before being taken out.

If the novice's budget permits it, the sacrifice is repeated for each Orisha represented in the Igbodu. After each decapitation, blood is poured into a salt-filled gourd, which is then set aside. It will be used to prepare the Orisha's Ashé. Each gourd is painted with the Orisha's emblematic color. There are no gourds for Obatala or for the spirits of the dead, who hate salt.

To clear the reek of blood from the air, the Babalawo spills a little water on the floor: *"iro ko suwo ogu osono."* Chorus: *"ero ero koise ero ariku babawa."*

The carcasses are skinned outside the Igbodu, and the skins are stretched on the floor. After the butchering, the pieces are piled on the hides. The offal is thrown up on the roof so that the vultures, Oshun's birds, may also enjoy the feast.

Each butchered animal is presented to the Orisha who demands its death. The topmost vertebra is taken out of the animal's head. This bone is added to the bundle of oracular cowrie shells handed to the Iyawo. It is proof that his Orisha drank the blood of a four-legged animal.

> After the big animals, it's time to sacrifice the birds. The Babalawo
> started with the roosters I'd bought.

Each rooster's head is cut off with a knife. Its blood is considered more powerful than that of the lesser birds, so it is mixed with the sheep's blood in the tureens. The Babalawo offers the bleeding bird to the Orisha: *"akuko mo kua ara aye."*

He then sacrifices the remaining birds by tearing off their heads with his bare hands: *"ko si cu ete eye otoko amu otoko epo."*

> Every time that he tore off the head of a bird, he put the stump
> in my mouth so I could drink some of the blood to make me
> stronger. His assistants also had a little bit from each bird.

Before each dead bird is removed from the Igbodu, its neck stump is joined to its legs and the Babalawo touches the floor three times: *"emi lo ku so osin ogun lo kua."*

All the feathers, except those of the ducks, are placed inside the tureens and mixed in with the blood and the sacred stones. The person nominated to clean the birds sings *"etie eku edeku etie eye adeya to lo ma likui ela popo ini eye"* while doing so.

The killing of the guinea hens ends the sacrificial ceremony. Before tearing off the head, the Babalawo twirls the bird above the novice's head: *"loricha fin fe to loricha fin fe to ara bobo loricha fin fe to ara bobo.* When it is dead, the Babalawo ends the ceremony: *"ero ko ishe."*

> That was it. I stayed seated on the "pilon," the blood dripping down
> my chest. The Babalawo's assistants brought in the heads of all
> the animals wrapped in their stomachs and put them in front of
> the Orishas.

22

For about an hour, the flesh and organs are left in the Igbodu as an offering before the Orishas' tureens. This allows the Orishas' essences, manifested in the sacred stones, to absorb the blood in which they have been soaking.

> The Babalawo fed his knife with coconuts. Everyone came in and pitched in to clean the room. All the blood was scrubbed from the floor and the splatters of blood on the walls were washed off.

After the Orishas have fed, the blood is washed off the stones with Omiero. The blood and the feathers must be disposed of in the manner favored by each Orisha: Yemaya's in the sea, Oshun's in a river, Elegua's at a crossroads, etc.

The preparations then begin for the feast that will be shared by all the participants except the Babalawo or Iyalocha who performed the sacrifices.

> That night, I slept on a mat laid out in front of the altar. One of the Iyalochas stayed with me to take care of me.

> When I woke up the next morning, the Babalawo gave me a little bit of smoked fish and some smoked jutia and three drinks of Omiero.

> I took off all my clothes again and got inside the tub of Omiero. After all the blood and everything had been washed off, I put on some new clothes, a yellow shirt and red pants, because those are Oshun's favorite colors.

> The Santeros helping him put on my collars. Then, the Babalawo painted my head again. He helped me sit on the "pilon." I sat there, barefoot all day long. All the Santeros and Santeras were sitting in front of me on a mat, clapping and laughing.

> All my friends and relatives came by and congratulated me and left money in a big gourd in front of me. So, that helped to pay for a lot of it.

The third day is reserved for the oracles that will guide the novice in his future path within Santeria.

> On the fourth day, right before I had to go back to work, I dressed up in my best white clothes, got into the rented limo with the Babalawo and his assistants, and went shopping. We bought baskets full of all the fruits and foods that Oshun likes and some food for the other Orishas, because it doesn't pay to make them jealous. Then, we took everything back to the house.

The Iyawo is now "married" to his Orisha. The initiation is over. He or she goes home. During the following year, life will not return to normal.

> Sleeping in separate beds is something my wife didn't like very much. But, I said, "Look, I have to do this. If I sleep with you, Oshun will kill me." Even if I were single, I couldn't be with a woman. That was the roughest part of the "asiento": I couldn't be with a woman for a year.

> I couldn't shake hands with anyone. Nobody could tell dirty jokes around me. I was pretty anti-social, let me tell you.

> I had to sleep with my head covered with a white handkerchief that whole year.

The novice will also wear white socks every day. He or she will change bed sheets every day. He or she will wear clean white clothes every day and change them immediately if they have become slightly soiled. Cleanliness is extremely important during the first year after the "asiento."

The women will not wear any makeup or shave their bodies. They are to avoid mirrors. They will have their own comb and will have a separate place in the house for all their personal objects, which no one must touch.

> I couldn't visit anyone who was sick or go to a funeral or a cemetery. The first three months were the hardest. I couldn't sit at the table

with my wife or with anyone else. I had to eat in the kitchen. And, I could only eat with my hands or with a spoon.

I couldn't go out at night. I couldn't go out in the rain. I almost got fired. I couldn't even take off my hat in the store.

Three months after my "asiento," I had to go get confirmed. I took all my tureens to the *Ile* [house where he was initiated] and went and did Ebo.

All the Otanes will be washed with their respective Ewes and offered fruits, sweets, and feathers. The Babalawo sacrifices birds.

In the afternoon, we fed the Orishas and gave them food, blood, and Moyuba. Everybody had a great time. We just ate and danced till dawn. When we are happy, the Orishas are happy.

By the time the last initiation *Ebo* comes around, a year has passed since the "asiento." In that time, the novice has had the responsibility to learn and follow the basic laws of Santeria:
How to attend his or her Orisha.
The offerings that belong to each Orisha.
The stories of each Orisha.
The Orisha's sacrificial animals.
How the animal is to be killed and cooked.
How to prepare the Igbodu for an initiation.
Memorize his or her "asiento" oracle and follow its advice.
Learn the responses to the chants and prayers.
Learn to perform the minor rituals.
Learn to throw the coconut shell oracle (Biague).
Learn to invoke the spirits of the dead, the Orishas, and the spirits of the elders (Moyuba).
Learn the ingredients needed for the rituals.
Learn his or her rights and responsibilities toward the elders in Santeria.

At the end of the year, I had to do another Ebo. It was more important than the three-month one, because it wasn't just a bird sacrifice. I had to feed the Orishas sheep and goats.

All the Santeros and Santeras that came to my "asiento" were invited, and I gave them each gifts and money.

At the end of twelve months, the Iyawo is considered a Santero or Santera. At that time, he or she is allowed to participate in an initiation and in the major rituals for the first time.

CHAPTER FOUR

The Gods (Orishas)

WE ARE THE GODS' CHILDREN. WHEN OLODUMARE SENDS OUT THE souls that will be born on this earth, the Orishas pick and choose among them, selecting the ones they wish for their own. They become our parents.

One does not choose an Orisha. The Orisha chooses his or her "child." Insisting on worshiping and being the "child" of an Orisha who has not recognized the initiate produces absolutely terrible results. The tales tell of physical and psychological disturbances leading to suicide.

No Santeria ceremony, no matter how simple, begins or ends without the ancestors being thanked and the spirits of the dead being placated. The dead are among us in a very intimate relationship. The ghost of an enemy in life is to be feared in death, having more power dead than alive.

The following are necessarily brief descriptions of the major Orishas and ancillary spirits. Geographical differences and inconsistencies in the names and natures of the Orishas are unavoidable in a religion without a written canon. But, it is diversity that has maintained Santeria alive through the centuries. The information is broken down into a few groupings.

The Saint: The Catholic persona assumed by the African deity to escape the wrath of the Inquisition.

The Day of the Week: Each Orisha has a favorite day. This is the most propitious time to make offerings, burn candles, consult the oracles, and perform the rites specified through the oracles.

Colors and Collars (Ilekes): Each Orisha owns a collar of a specific color and shape. The Orisha's "child" must wear it around his or her neck. The collars should not be kept in the pocket or purse or inside a balled-up handkerchief. Care should be taken that they remain unsnarled. When they are not being worn, they should be placed on the

Orisha's tureen. When there are no tureens, they should be carefully laid out on a white cloth.

The collars are not to be lent to anyone. A Santero or Santera should never sleep, have sex, or shower with them on.

An Orisha's colors are the same as those of the beads that make up his or her Ileke. The Orisha's "child" should wear clothes in the colors that are pleasing to his or her patron. The Orisha's tureen and implements should also be of the appropriate color.

Sacrificial Animals: Each Orisha prefers to feed on the blood of a particular group of animals. His or her sacrifices should consist of those animals.

Sacrificial Food: Like their worshipers, Orishas have their favorite foods and are extremely pleased to have them presented as offerings.

Herbs: Each Orisha has power over a group of healing and magical herbs. The Omiero used to wash the Orisha's Otanes should be made up of the herbs that "belong" to the Orisha.

The most common recourse for a Santero or any believer in Santeria, when confronted by a problem whose solution does not require an animal sacrifice or any other specific Ebo, is to prepare an herb bath (Ewe). Used externally as a body cleanser, a spirit cleanser, or to clean the house and internally as medicinal potions, herb baths are the most economical and fastest method for resolving problems and dissipating evils.

When working with herbs for various Orishas, it is important that the herbs be piled separately until they are ready to be mixed in the final Omiero. Worshipers also often wash in their Orisha's Omiero to regain their health or to cleanse themselves from impurities.

The herbs for the Ewe or the entire Omiero should be prepared in a deep mortar or over the soup tureen belonging to the Orisha being petitioned. They are never boiled and never used dry. The Otanes may be washed as frequently and as thoroughly as the person invoking the Orisha feels is needed.

As the stones are being washed, a Moyuba should be made to the Orisha that is being washed. Animal sacrifices are not required before or after the stones are cleaned.

Ornaments: The "tools" used by the Orishas and their worshipers to focus their power.

Apataki: These are the traditional African tales of the Orishas and their relationships among themselves and with men. They make up a constantly shifting mosaic of loves, betrayals, and intrigue.

And, a note about the music that always accompanies the ceremonies: The drum is the music of the African gods. Everything in Santeria is done to the beat of the sacred drums. They take the worshipers' messages to the Orishas.

When the Orishas grant a request, the drums are played in thanksgiving and in joy. They are also played next to the sickbed, at funerals, and for the spirits of the dead.

Regardless of the occasion, the drums must be well fed and honored before and after they are played. The offerings are made to Osain, the Orisha who "owns" the drums. When the drums are fed and happy, they sound better.

Olodumare (Olofin, Olorun)

Saint: Jesus Christ or the dove of the Holy Spirit.
Day of the Week: Thursday.
Colors and Collars (Ilekes): All and none.
Sacrificial Animal: None. No animal sacrifices of any type.
Sacrificial Food: None.
Herbs: None.
Ornaments: None.
Apataki: Olodumare, even though he was king of the other gods, had a mortal fear of mice. The other gods thought that a king, especially their king, should not be afraid of anything as unimportant and weak as a mouse.

"Olodumare has turned into a weak old woman," they said, for they believed it shameful to fear mice. "It's time that we took away his power and named another king." Besides, they wanted total dominion of the world.

Things continued as they were until the principal Orishas got together again. "We must take away Olodumare's power," they said. "He is getting old and weak."

Everyone agreed, again. There was a problem, though. Olodumare was old, but he certainly was not weak. He was fierce and terrible, and not one of the other Orishas would dare to challenge him in combat.

The Orishas thought and talked and thought some more until one, no one knows who, came up with an idea. "Let's scare Olodumare to death," said the unknown Orisha.

"How do you propose to do that?" asked the other Orishas, since they themselves were deathly afraid of Olodumare.

"Olodumare is afraid of mice," said the Orisha.

"Everyone knows that," exclaimed the disappointed Orishas. "We thought that you had an idea."

"If he is afraid of one mouse," continued the Orisha, "what would happen if we invite him over to our house and fill it with mice?"

"Tell us," said the other Orishas.

"If Olodumare finds himself in a house full of mice, he will be so afraid that he will run away from here or die. We'll take over his house, and we will be the masters of the world."

"That's a wonderful plan," they all exclaimed. Putting their heads together, the Orishas began to plot how they were going to lure Olodumare to their house and scare him to death with mice.

They forgot that Elegua was by the door. He lived by the door, since he is the Orisha that rules roads, routes, and entrances. They had forgotten all about him. He heard all their plans.

What did Elegua do? What did the trickster Orisha do? He knew the day that Olodumare was coming. He had listened to the other Orishas' plans. He waited and hid behind the door.

Olodumare arrived, happy to have been invited to a party. He knew that he was not as popular among the Orishas as he used to be. Little did he know that the other Orishas were hidden, waiting to release hundreds of mice. The moment he stepped inside, the door was slammed shut at Olodumare's back. The mice were released.

Olodumare was terrified and ran around the house screaming, "The mice are attacking. The mice are attacking!"

He tried to find a place to hide, but every box he opened and every closet he ran into just had more and more mice. Olodumare ran head first at the door, ready to demolish it, just so that he could escape the tormenting rodents. Just as head and door were going to meet, Elegua stepped out and stopped his panicked rush.

"Stop, Olodumare," said Elegua, putting his arms around the terrified old Orisha. "No mouse will harm you."

"Yes, they will. Yes, they will," cried Olodumare.

"Watch," said Elegua. He started eating the mice.

Elegua ate and ate and ate until he had eaten all the mice.

Olodumare, whose fear had turned to fury, demanded, "Who dared do this to me?"

Elegua said nothing. Smiling like a happy cat, he pointed out the hiding places of all the plotting Orishas.

Olodumare immediately punished them in a very terrible and painful manner. After he grew tired of watching them hop and scream, he turned to Elegua and said, "Now, what can I do for you?"

Elegua scuffed the floor and shook his head. "Oh, nothing," he said.

"Nothing!" roared Olodumare. "You saved me and you saved my crown and you want nothing?"

"Well," said Elegua, "maybe just a little thing."

"You can have whatever you want," said Olodumare firmly.

"I want the right to do what I want," said Elegua. He went on with more conviction, ignoring Olodumare's raised eyebrows. "I want the right to do what I will. I want the right to do what I want, whatever that may be."

Olodumare wished it so, and so it was. From that moment on, Elegua is the only god who does as he wills without restraints or limits.

Notes: Olodumare is unique within the Yoruba pantheon. He never comes down to earth. Few Santeros speak of Olodumare because there are no Babalawos "asentados" in him. No one is "asentado" in Olodumare. He never possesses anyone at a "bembe" or a "golpe de Santo."

He is the ruler of all the other gods, except Elegua, as the Apataki shows. More than the Orishas' ruler, he was their creator as well as the source and origin of men, animals, plants, rivers, oceans, and the heavens. He also created the earth, the sun, the moon, and the stars.

Before going to bed, a Santero will ask Olodumare to give him the strength to get up the following day by chanting, *"olofin ewa wo"* ("May Olofin help us get up").

At dawn, when he awakens and ascertains that he is still among the living, he says, *"olodumare e egbeo"* ("May Olodumare grant us a good day").

Olodumare is old. He is very tired and has been working long and hard on the universe, which is a very large job. He should not be bothered with small things. Santeros ask favors of the Orishas who can directly solve their problems and do not bother Olodumare.

A series of commandments are attributed to Olodumare: You will not steal. You will not kill except in self defense or to survive. You will not eat human flesh. You will live in peace with your neighbor. You will not covet your neighbor's possessions. You will not use my name in vain. You will honor your mother and your father. You will not ask for more than I am able to give you, and you will be satisfied with your destiny. You will not fear death or take your own life. You will respect and obey my laws. You will teach these commandments to your son.

Obatala

Saint: Our Lady of Mercy (La Virgen de las Mercedes).

Day of the Week: Sunday. Thursday is also popular.

Colors and Collars (Ilekes): His color is the purest white. The collar is made up of all white beads. A variation on the collar is twenty-one white beads followed by a coral bead repeated to make up the desired length.

Sacrificial Animals: Female goats, white chickens, white canaries. In cases of grave illness, he will accept a white female calf.

Sacrificial Foods: Yam, rice flour paste, corn meal dumplings, and black-eyed peas. He hates alcoholic beverages. The only spice that Obatala likes is cocoa butter. He drinks chequete. His water comes from the rain. His favorite fruit is the sweet soursop (guanabana).

Herbs: Amansa guapo, chamise (wild cane), madonna lilies, calla lilies, cotton, purslane, almonds, white hamelia, white elderberry, white peonies, sweet basil, sweet soursop, wild mint, marjoram, jimson weed, blite, goosefoot, African bayonet, yucca, witch hazel, and sweet balm among others.

Ornaments: Obatala's image must be made of white metal or silver. In one hand, he holds a crown. A sun, a moon, four wristlets, a walking stick with a clenched fist, a half moon and a coiled snake—all made out of silver. Two ivory eggs.

Apataki: Obatala was the only Orisha who knew where Olodumare lived. This gave him a very important position among the other Orishas. At that time, the Orishas had no power of their own. They had to beg all their power from Olodumare.

"Obatala!" the Orishas would call out. "Please have Olodumare straighten out the fight between Oshun and Chango."

And, Obatala would make the long journey to Olodumare's house and relay the message.

"Obatala, a person needs healing and love," said Yemaya. "Please have Olodumare give me the power to heal him."

Back and forth traveled Obatala. He gave messages. He granted favors. He ran himself ragged. He became unhappy. He was not ambitious, and he knew that the other Orishas were talking behind his back.

"Obatala thinks he is our leader," the Orishas grumbled. "He gives himself airs just because he knows where Olodumare lives."

"Do you see how he listens to us?" complained another Orisha. "It's as if we were his spoiled children. Who does he think he is?"

So Obatala took all the Orishas to Olodumare's home.

"Good morning, Obatala," said Olodumare. "What can I do for your friends?"

"I'm tired of running back and forth, with all due respect," said Obatala. "I would like for you to give each of my friends some of your power."

"I don't know," Olodumare hemmed and hawed. "Do you think it's the right thing to do?"

"Just think, great Lord," said Obatala. "If you give them a bit of your power, I would not have to come here and bother you about this and that every day."

"You have a point there, Obatala," said Olodumare. "I'll do it."

So, Olodumare gave each of the Orishas a bit of his power, hoping to get a little peace and quiet. Finally, he got to Obatala.

"To you, Obatala," he said, "I give the right to control the heads of all the human beings."

Since it is the head that makes a human being good or evil, a good son or a bad son, Obatala became the Orisha with the most authority over human beings. More than any of the other Orishas.

"Did you see that?" said the other Orishas. "He brought us here just so that he could maintain his power."

Which just goes to prove that you can't please anyone.

Notes: Obatala is the supreme divinity on the terrestrial plane. He represents such a refined purity that it cannot be described through words or songs. He is reason and justice and all that is moral.

Controlling the head, he is considered the father of all human beings. He gives the best advice and is the one to turn to in times of great difficulties.

The relationship between the Santeros and the Orishas is much more intimate and direct than in other religions. The Orishas have human passions and desires. They can be cruel and unjust just like human beings. When the Orishas manifest their cruelty, Obatala is called upon to mediate in the situation and to calm and soothe the furious Orisha.

Orunmila (Ifa, Orula)

Saint: St. Francis.

Day of the Week: Thursday. Sunday is also popular.

Colors and Collars (Ilekes): His colors are green and yellow. The collar is made up of alternating green and yellow beads strung to the desired length.

Sacrificial Animals: A goat who has not given birth. Dark chickens.

Sacrificial Foods: Red snapper and yam puree. Plums are his favorite fruit. He drinks white wine, and his water is to come from a spring. His favorite condiment is corojo butter.

Herbs: Guava, sage, nightshade, ginger, dog bane, guanine, myrtle, corn, honeysuckle, night jasmine, pitch apple, guasima (guazuma guazuma: a tree native to Cuba), parami, and corojo among others.

Ornaments: A hardwood board having various shapes according to the Babalawos' tradition (Ifa's Board). As well as serving as a surface upon which the cowrie shell oracle is cast, the board is the table upon which many rites are performed. Cowrie shells and oracular collars also belong to Orunmila.

Apataki: Orunmila does not fear death. One day, a woman came running up to Orunmila. These were the days when the Orishas still walked on the earth. She clutched at his shoulders and cried out, "Iku is going around and around my house."

This was very serious because Iku is the name of death. When Iku wants someone, she walks outside the house looking for a small hole or opening through which she can get in and take away the person inside.

"Iku is at my house," she cried again. "She wants to take my only son, my little boy. Iku sent in a fever, and it's going to kill him if I don't do something." She started to drag Orunmila back to her house. "We have to hurry," she said, sobbing. "I have turned my back. Iku may be getting into my house right now to take away my child."

Orunmila smiled down at her and said, "Don't cry, good woman."

"But what should I do? You have to help me," she said.

Orunmila patted her head to calm her down. "Don't worry," he said. "Go to the market and buy three baskets full of okra and take them back to your house."

"What about my child?" sobbed the frightened woman. "I will go to your house and make sure that Iku does not go in," said Orunmila. "Go to the market in peace."

The woman followed Orunmila's advice. She went to the market and bought three heaping baskets of okra. When she got home, breathless from having run with the three baskets, she found Orunmila waiting for her.

"Here are the baskets," she said. "What are you going to do with them?"

"Hush," said Orunmila. "I don't have time for explanations."

He took the baskets from the woman, went inside the house, and spread the contents of the baskets all over the floors until they were covered by a thick carpet of okra.

He handed the baskets back to the anxious mother. "Don't worry, mother," he said. "Iku won't be able to do your son any harm."

Exhausted by the run from the market and a fear and anxiety that had not let her sleep for days, the mother collapsed on a cot and went to sleep.

As she slept, the child's fever rose. Iku was thinking that it was time to take the child away, so she made the sickness worse. Iku went up to the door and found that it was unlatched and had not closed all the way. Death slipped in through the crack, hurrying to get to the child before the mother awoke.

Iku strode across the room with her usual firm and silent steps. But, when her hard and bony heels stepped on the okra, the fruit burst open. Iku slipped and slid. All the okra on the floor oozed its sap as Iku slipped from one side of the room to the other. The sap was as slippery as soap. Both of death's feet slipped out from under her. Her long arm bones windmilled trying to regain her balance.

"Oh, crap," she cried. And, before she could say anything else, her bony hips hit the floor, shaking loose all her joints.

Iku had to slip and dig through the mess of okra to find one or two little bones that had come off. She made her way very carefully to the door. Outside, Orunmila waited for her.

"How are you this afternoon, Iku?" he asked very politely.

"Curse you, Orunmila," she spat. "I know that this is all your fault. Curse you and that cursed woman in there for getting you to help her."

"Are you coming again?" Orunmila called out as Iku hobbled off down the path.

She turned and gave him an evil look.

"Are you crazy?" she said. "I'm going to wait a long time and make sure that okra is gone."

Notes: Orunmila is highly regarded within the Santeria pantheon. The Orisha who predicts the future, he is in charge of destiny, both human and Orishan.

He is an invisible presence at every birth, since he also oversees pregnancies and the care and raising of children. He knows how to use the ceremonial and healing herbs and instructs human beings in their uses. Orunmila is the intermediary between humans and Olodumare.

The Santeros and the Babalawos are familiar with the problems and tragedies that afflict human beings. Thanks to Orunmila, who communicates with them through the oracles, the Babalawo or the Santero can come up with the solution to a person's problems. Their advice must be followed to the letter.

Orunmila never possesses a human being. It is felt that he is too important and close to Olodumare for that. In a Santeria ceremony, the Iyalochas of Oshun dance for him since he does not have a physical body that can enjoy the drumming and dancing.

CHAPTER FIVE

The Gods (cont.)

Elegua

SAINT: THE HOLY CHILD OF ATOCHA.

Day of the Week: Monday and the third day of each month.

Colors and Collars (Ilekes): Red and black. His collar is made up of three red beads followed by three black beads. After the three black beads, a red bead alternates with a black bead three times. The sequence is repeated until the desired length is obtained.

Sacrificial Animals: Small goats, roosters. On rare occasions, monkeys, sheep, bulls, ox, and deer. Chickens should not be offered. Elegua is a glutton and will bother and torment the participants at a ceremony until he has had his fill of blood.

Sacrificial Foods: Smoked fish and smoked jutia. He loves yams. His favorite fruit is sugar cane. Everything should be well spiced with corojo butter. He loves to drink aguardiente, and he favors standing water.

Herbs: Abre camino (*bunchosia media*), Cuban spurge, sargasso, wild convulvulus, foxtail, nettles, manyroot, crowfoot, neat's tongue, white pine nuts, jack bean, spiny blite, nightshade, black-eyed peas, ateje (*cordia collocea*), heliotrope, pigeon peas, mastic tree, camphor leaves, chili peppers, cornstalks, corn leaves, and corn silk, avocado leaves, avocado roots, coconut husk, coconut palm stem, corojo, guava, wild croton, coffee, cowhage, peppergrass, dried rose buds, senna, soapberry tree, bitter bush, and mint among others.

Ornaments: Elegua is never without his "garabato," the shepherd's hook (sometimes only a crooked stick or club) with which he metes out punishment. To protect temples, cities, and houses, he resides in a helmet-shaped construction made out of stone or cement with cowrie shells for eyes. The small statue is placed next to an entrance way. From this abode, Elegua protects all the residents. Since he is as playful as a child, tops, marbles, and kites hold a special fascination for him.

Apataki: Orunmila had returned to earth to see how all the Babalawos he had trained in the arts of divination were getting along. He decided to travel from town to town and greet his old students.

"Orunmila, how nice to see you," said one. "I don't have time to talk with you now; I have an appointment."

"Orunmila, how are you?" said another. "If you come back on Wednesday, I'll be able to see you."

"Orunmila, I'm very busy with my clients right now," said a third. "Could you come back in a day or so?"

Orunmila was furious. All his old students were ignoring him. They were too concerned with making money and having a big reputation to honor their old teacher. Orunmila decided to teach them a lesson.

He sent out notice that he would challenge all the Babalawos to a contest to see who cast the most accurate oracles. Orunmila figured that, after they had been shamed by his incomparable skill, all the Babalawos would respect him again.

After the notices had been sent, he went to the nearest town and challenged the Babalawo. Orunmila proved to be a far better reader of the oracles, of course. But the Babalawo refused to pay Orunmila the agreed upon amount.

Elegua, who is never far away and always likes to play tricks, walked up to Orunmila and the Babalawo.

"Hello, Orunmila, how are you today?" said Elegua.

"I am angry, Elegua," fumed Orunmila.

"And why is that, dear Orunmila?" Elegua tried to stifle his giggles, since he knew perfectly well what had been going on.

"This cheat of a Babalawo has lost a wager with me," answered Orunmila. "And now he refuses to pay."

Elegua looked up and down the nervous Babalawo. "Is that right? Are you trying to cheat Orunmila?"

"Well, Lord Elegua. . ." stammered the Babalawo.

Before he could say another word, Elegua reached out and put his powerful warrior's hand around the Babalawo's neck. He looked at the man straight in the eye.

"Tell me," he said softly, "are you looking for trouble?"

"No," squeaked the Babalawo.

Elegua raised his garabato stick over the Babalawo's head.

"You'd never do anything to make me angry, would you?" growled Elegua.

Another squeak, "No."

"And what are you going to do?" asked Elegua, tapping the unhappy Babalawo on the nose with his garabato stick.

"I'm going to pay Orunmila?" asked the Babalawo.

"What was that?" shouted Elegua, shaking the Babalawo back and forth.

"I'm going to pay Orunmila. I'm going to pay Orunmila," stuttered the Babalawo.

He took his money pouch out of his clothes and handed the whole thing over to Orunmila.

"I thought you wanted to cheat Orunmila, but I see that you are a man who pays his debts when he loses," said Elegua and gave the Babalawo a resounding slap on the back. "I'll leave you alone."

Orunmila and Elegua turned and walked away arm in arm. The Babalawo picked himself up from the road and began dusting off his clothes.

"One more thing," said Elegua, turning back to the Babalawo.

"Yes?" the Babalawo cringed.

"Since you have forgotten that the oracles are meant to communicate with the Orishas and not to increase the Babalawo's wealth, I'm prohibiting you from using the Dilogun ever again."

Orunmila and Elegua left the Babalawo wailing after them. In the next town, the Babalawo saw Elegua and his stick standing next to Orunmila. There was no trouble there.

Notes: Elegua is the guardian of entrances, roads, and paths. He is the first Orisha to be invoked in a ceremony and the last one to be bid farewell. He has to be first in anything, just like a spoiled child. The first rhythms of the drums belong to him. He must be petitioned before all the oracles. Orunmila is the one who communicates, but Elegua guards the paths of communication. It is he who acts as an intermediary between human beings and the other Orishas.

As the trickster, he is feared because, with so much power controlled only by his whim, great harm may result from his practical jokes. Like a very large and powerful child, he is ruthless with those who cross his path when he is in the midst of a tantrum. If his precedence is not carefully maintained and the proper ceremonies are not followed, Elegua becomes indignant and rushes to open the paths to Iku, death.

All beings have their destinies, but through Elegua's influence, destiny and luck may be changed. However, when petitioning Elegua, the Santero must always remember that he is a trickster and word the request very carefully. He can just as easily block the path to happiness and luck as open it.

Elegua appears to travelers as a small child with the face of an old man, wearing a Panama hat and smoking a good cigar. He takes on other guises in order to play his tricks and to measure the level of charity and compassion among human beings.

When Elegua possesses a Santero, he immediately heads to the door and stands guard. There, he carries out his pranks and childish mischief, dancing and threatening the other participants with a smack from his garabato stick.

Elegua is one of the fiercest warriors in the Yoruba pantheon. When he joins with Ogun and Oshosi in battle, nothing can stand in their way.

HOW TO MAKE AN ELEGUA

No matter which branch of the Santeria tradition is followed, Elegua always inhabits a stone. It could be a natural stone or a cement form. These are the instructions for constructing an Elegua out of natural stone.

Find a medium-sized stone; one about the size and shape of a large potato is ideal. The stone should be collected next to a railroad track, at a crossroads, or under a coconut palm.

Find the natural base of the stone, the surface where it will come to rest upright by itself. Bore a perfectly round hole into the base of the stone about two inches deep by an inch in diameter.

Cut the head off a white chicken and let the blood drip onto the stone. Make an Omiero with May rain water, coconut milk, and the herbs that belong to Elegua. Wash the stone thoroughly in the Omiero and leave it to soak for twenty-four hours.

Select three small precious stones. All gems belong to Elegua. Place the three gems in the hole in the stone along with three small pieces of silver, three small nuggets of gold, three small pieces of coconut, some feathers from the sacrificed chicken, and a small personal piece of gold jewelry.

Seal the hole with cement made with sand from a crossroads, guinea pepper, and cemetery dust. When the cement is dry, paint the rock black. Crown it with a fighting cock's spur, with the curve toward the back. Give it cowrie shell eyes.

Take a white rooster and the rock to a palm tree growing by a crossroads. Sacrifice the rooster and let the blood drip on the stone. Bury the rooster three inches deep at the base of the palm.

After three days, dig up the rooster and wash it in a flowing river, first asking Oshun's permission by tossing a live white chicken into the river along with a little honey. Elegua is ready to be stationed by the door.

HOW TO PLACE AN ELEGUA

Monday is the most auspicious day to position the Elegua, but it can be done on any day of the week.

Place the Elegua inside a large clay pot heavily smeared on the outside with corojo butter and place the pot next to the door. Smear the lintel and the door with corojo butter. Sacrifice a young white rooster and allow the blood to drip upon the stone. Make three balls of uncooked corn meal and honey. Place them next to the stone along with a gourd of aguardiente, cigars, pieces of coconut, a small plate of sweets, smoked jutia, and as many of the things that are pleasing to Elegua as the Santero is able to afford. Arrange all the offerings around the pot.

Kiss the neck of the sacrificed rooster. Consult the coconut oracle and see if Elegua is happy with all his offerings. If Elegua responds favorably, this is the best time to consult the oracle about anything else that may be worrying you.

Elegua's food should be changed every Monday. A candle should be lit in his honor every time he is fed.

Elegua's presence is felt in the house as a noise that runs from one side of the door to the other. He is often seen by small children, who can touch him and exchange toys. Only those persons who have been initiated into Santeria and have been possessed by an Orisha have the power to empower an Elegua.

HOW TO SALUTE AN ELEGUA

Stand before the Elegua. Lift your right arm and move your right foot out to the side and say: *"A elegua ako pashu eshu toru le fi ya yomare ako eshu tori toru tere mafun elegua laroye locua e elegua atande naro elegua maferefun elegua."* Or, you may speak your own language. The Orisha will understand the greeting.

Repeat the same process with the left arm and foot. When you are finished, turn your back on the Elegua and wipe your feet backwards as if you were cleaning them. Never kneel to or lie down in front of an Elegua.

AN EBO TO ELEGUA

Three pieces of yellow paper or three small paper grocery bags
Corojo butter   Three pieces of smoked fish   Smoked jutia
Dried corn   Cinnamon sticks   Three small pieces of coconut
Three cigars   Honey   Nine pennies

Divide the offering evenly among the three small bags or the pieces of paper. Wrap each small package tightly with red and black thread.

Pass each packet over your head three times, turning around three times after each pass. Repeat the procedure over your feet, hands, and, finally, all over your body.

Throw away one package at a crossroads. Throw the second away in a lot or field full of tall weeds. Throw the last one away near a cemetery.

Chango (Jakuta, Obakoso)

Saint: St. Barbara.

Day of the Week: Saturday. Friday is also popular. Huge parties are held in Chango's honor on December 4, St. Barbara's day according to the Catholic calendar.

Colors and Collars (Ilekes): His colors are red and white. The collar is made up of six red beads followed by six white beads. Then, a red bead alternates with a white bead six times. The sequence is repeated until the desired length is obtained.

Sacrificial Animals: Roosters. Complicated Ebos may require sheep, small bulls, pigs, goats, deer, rabbits, and oxen. A horse is required to remove a very strong curse or to change an oracle predicting death.

Sacrificial Foods: Chango is a glutton. He loves huge portions of corn meal and okra. Apples are his favorite fruit, and he likes pitahaya (cactus fruit). All his food should be heavily loaded with corojo butter. Chango drinks red wine in large quantities. His water should come from a pond.

Herbs: Banyan tree, kapok tree, poplar, sorghum, clematis, hog plum, Cuban spurge, cashews, ironwood, mugwort, bran, climbing vines, bull's testicles, American spurge, leeks, pitahaya, plantains and bananas, red hamelias, Bermuda grass, royal palm, pine, lignum vitae, amansa guapo, pine nuts, and apple trees among others.

Ornaments: A sword, a knife, a machete, an ax, a dagger, and a spear, almost always made out of cedar. Chango is also represented by the image of a warrior holding a large double-edged hatchet in one hand and a sword in the other. Both images, the warrior and St. Barbara, can be found on the same altar.

Apataki: Obakoso, in Yoruba, means "the king that did not hang himself." This is the story of how Chango came by that name.

Chango has always been a womanizer. Back in the days when he was a king in Africa, he had two wives. He ruled his women hard and he ruled his kingdom hard, for his temper had not mellowed yet with age.

"You are always yelling and stomping in this house," said Wife Number One.

"That's right," said Wife Number Two, "You never have a kind word for anyone."

"All you care about is your stomach," said Wife Number One.

"And you don't care about us," said Wife Number Two.

"You never buy us presents," said Wife Number One.

"You never take us anywhere," said Wife Number Two.

"You don't love us," wailed both wives in unison.

"I don't stomp around the house," shouted Chango, stomping around the house. "I was having a pleasant morning, thinking about how nice it would be to have a little wild duck, and you two have ruined it."

"Do you hear that?" said Wife Number One to Wife Number Two. "I told you all he cared about was his stomach."

"That's it!" shouted Chango. "I'm getting on my horse and riding into the forest. At least no one will nag me there."

"How long are you going to be gone?" asked Wife Number One.

"I'll be back when I'm good and ready. Don't bother looking for me or coming after me," snarled Chango.

"As if we would," sniffed Wife Number Two.

Chango stormed off through the palace, slamming doors and kicking cats. No one paid him any attention, since this was his normal way of walking through the castle. All his subjects were used to Chango's tantrums. No one waved as Chango rode off into the forest.

"He's in one of his moods," said the groom to a kitchen maid. "He'll be back in a little while." He rubbed the top of his head. "I hope he comes back in a better mood and does not hit me again."

A week passed and Chango had not come back.

"He's with a new woman," some said.

"He is on an adventure," said others.

"He's drunk somewhere," said Wife Number One.

A month passed. Chango's wives would burst out crying without reason. His subjects missed the noise of the slamming doors and the screeching cats.

"Where can he be?" they asked.

"He's been gone way too long," said others.

"We have to go and look for him," said Wife Number Two. "I can't stand this any longer."

A well-organized search party was sent out into the forest. It returned a week later.

"Well?" asked Wife Number One.

"Nothing," said the captain of the search party.

Rumors began to fly in the palace.

"Chango went into the forest and hung himself because he was ashamed of what a bad king he was," said some people.

"He tied a rope around his neck and jumped off the top of a large banyan tree because his mistress abandoned him," said others.

The rumors and the search parties kept coming and going. Chango was not to be found. It had been six months since he had ridden off into the forest.

A new massive search was organized. Everyone in the palace, from the youngest child to the oldest woman, set out into the forest. They looked under every stone. They climbed every tree. Slowly, they made their way into the center of the forest.

Hundreds of voices cried out, "Chango! Where are you, Chango?" And the echo came back, "Chango."

Women beat their breasts and smeared their bodies with ashes. "Where are you, Chango?" they shouted. "Tell us if you have hung yourself."

Deep in the deepest part of the forest, up on top of the tallest and oldest banyan tree, Chango woke up from a nap. He heard the hundreds of voices that had awakened him. "Chango, Chango. Where are you, Chango?"

Chango was furious. He hated noise, and he especially hated it when it woke him up from a nap.

"What is that racket?" he shouted. "Who are all you people?"

Then he saw that it was hundreds of his warriors and thousands of his subjects beating the bushes, scaring the animals and destroying the peace and quiet of the forest. Chango got angrier, as most people do when they are rudely awakened from a nap. He stood up on the topmost branch of the banyan tree and roared, "I am here! I did not hang myself, and I will never hang myself."

The forest was silent. A thousand heads looked up to Chango, standing proudly on top of the banyan tree.

"Come down, Chango, come down!" shouted his subjects.

"Quiet," yelled Chango. He waited for all the murmuring and muttering and crying to die out. "I'm not coming down," he said. "If I come down, if I go back to the palace, my wives," he pointed a stiff and slightly dirty finger at them, "who are now friends, crying over my loss, will start fighting with each other again. What's worse, they'll start fighting with me again."

"No, we won't," shouted Wife Number One.

"You get yourself right down here," said Wife Number Two.

"Come down, Chango. Come down," shouted all his subjects.

Chango sat on the branch and thought about what he should do. He thought and thought until all the shouting had died down again.

"Are you coming down now?" asked Wife Number One.

"It's almost time for dinner," said Wife Number Two.

Chango came to a decision. He stood on the branch atop the banyan tree. He raised his arms and shouted, "My people!"

"Come down, Chango," they all cried.

"Quiet!" shouted Chango. "I've come to the conclusion that it is just too much of a bother and a problem and a headache to try to govern all of you."

"Are you calling us a problem?" shrieked Wife Number One.

"Are you saying we're a headache?" screamed Wife Number Two.

"From now on," said Chango, as he dodged a couple of well-aimed rocks thrown by his wives, "I will still rule you, but I will rule you from far away." Another rock whizzed by his head. "From very far away. I'm going to rule you from the sky."

Ignoring the shouts and tears of his subjects and the curses and stones from his wives, Chango grabbed a thick chain that led from the top of the banyan tree to the sky. He pulled himself up link by link. When he paused for breath and looked down, his subjects were tiny. He could not distinguish his wives. He looked up. The chain disappeared into the blue sky.

He climbed and he climbed and he climbed until he reached the sky. There he stayed.

He is now an Orisha among the Orishas. Chango looks at the actions of his people down here on earth and is swift in his punishment of the unjust and of those who do not follow the religion or make the sacrifices.

He hurls down deadly thunderbolts on those people. He makes whole cities explode, or he blows them away in terrible tropical storms. His angry words make whole trees go up in flames, and his annoyed snorts create wind storms that sweep all that displeases him away forever.

Notes: Chango is the most popular and the most widely known Orisha in Santeria. He rules violent storms and thunder and also reconciles these forces into peace and understanding. Like a tropical storm, Chango's attacks are sudden and devastating but are soon over.

During "golpe de Santos" (Santeria ceremonies), Chango descends among the participants and dances with his followers, holding his feared two-edged sword. When he possesses someone, the "caballo" dances round and round like a top. The possessed Santero will take food to all the other participants in the ceremony. Chango will then demand a sacrifice from those who have eaten.

Chango loves good music, dancing, and drumming. He likes to have fun but is a braggart who provokes violent situations. He loves women and encourages clandestine sexual adventures among his "children."

Chango has three wives: Oba, Oya (who used to be Ogun's wife), and Oshun. Yemaya is his adoptive mother. When Chango becomes aroused, it's necessary to beg his three wives and his adoptive mother to intervene. The only Orishas Chango respects are Elegua and Olodumare.

Chango's "children" are recognized at birth by the image of a cross on their tongues. These children cannot have their hair cut until they are twelve, or they will lose their power to see into the future. They are known as the *Bamboche,* the messengers of Chango.

Oshun

Saint: Our Lady of Charity (La Caridad del Cobre), Cuba's patron Saint.

Day of the Week: Saturday. It is the day when lovers must act if they want their love returned.

Colors and Collars (Ilekes): Coral and amber. The collar is strung with yellow and red beads. Amber and coral are to be used if the Santero has the money. The collar is made up of five amber beads followed by five coral beads. Then, one amber bead alternates with one coral bead five times. The pattern is repeated to obtain the desired length.

Sacrificial Animals: Neutered or female goat, white chickens, sheep, female calf, female pig, female rabbit. Oshun does not like any other type of bird. Her sacrifices should be made next to rivers or other sources of flowing sweet water.

Sacrificial Foods: *Ochin-Ochin* (spinach with shrimp) and pumpkins. Her fruit is the lucuma. All of her food should be liberally garnished with honey. Oshun drinks chamomile tea. The water for the tea, and all water used in a ceremony for Oshun, should be river water.

All offerings to Oshun must be extremely clean and well-prepared. She will not enter a dirty house.

Herbs: Rose, sunflowers, Indian lotus, male and female ferns, creeping crowfoot, purslane, oranges and orange leaves, papaya, amber, anise seed and flower, peppergrass, marigold, sow thistle, river weeds, seaweed, white hamelias, plantain, vervain, lantana, purple grapes, maidenhair fern, rosemary, wild lettuce.

Ornaments: Copper is Oshun's metal, and she is sometimes represented by a gourd crowned by festive feathers and filled with copper pennies. She also loves gold, and her chief ornament consists of a golden crown with five points. From the points hang five rays, five spears, or five arrows. Oshun also owns two oars, a bell, and five bracelets. She loves fans made of peacock feathers.

Apataki: Oshun is now married to Chango. Her first husband was Orunmila.

Oshun was the most breathtaking, absolutely beautiful maiden in the region when she was a young girl. Hundreds of suitors would come seeking to marry her. But the result would always be the same.

"Marry me," gasped or shouted or whispered the suitor.

And Oshun would turn her back and walk away from the young man. His last sight of Oshun would be her exquisite hips swinging back and forth, disappearing into her mother's house.

More and more suitors showed up at Oshun's house, bringing mountains of gifts. Their horses trampled the garden. Finally, after seeing her rose bushes eaten by a camel, Oshun's mother rushed out of the house shouting, "That's enough!" The serenaders stopped playing in mid-chord. The duelists dropped their swords.

"You get out of my garden right now!" shouted Oshun's mother. "And don't come this way again."

A brave suitor spoke up. "We're in love with your daughter."

"That's right," said another. "We're here to win her hand."

"You're here making my life miserable," grumbled Oshun's mother. However, she realized that they were right in wooing her daughter, since she was the greatest beauty in the region.

"You're in the right," she told the surprised suitor. "But," she added, raising her voice to be heard by the crowd of suitors, "this madness has got to stop."

"But we want to marry your daughter," they wailed.

"Quiet!" shouted Oshun's mother. "I have determined a fair way for all of you to compete for my daughter's hand without tearing around in my flowers and vegetables."

The crowd settled down.

"My daughter's name is secret. Only I know it. The one who finds out what her name is will have proven that he has the cunning to win my daughter's hand in marriage. His skill will melt her heart and will win my approval. He will be her husband."

Orunmila was in the crowd of suitors. He is the god of oracles and can see the future.

"This should be easy," he said to himself, concentrating.

But, no matter what he did or how many times he threw the coconuts or rattled the cowrie shells, Orunmila was unable to find out the name of the most beautiful girl in the region.

Orunmila's other attribute is wisdom. He knew when to call for help. He went out in search of Elegua and found the trickster Orisha. Even though he was only Orunmila's porter, Elegua had taught him all the sciences and secrets of divination.

"Elegua, old friend, you must help me," cried Orunmila, seizing Elegua by the shoulders.

"Do you need money?" asked Elegua.

"I'm in love and I need your help," said Orunmila.

"Even worse," said Elegua.

"Please help me find the name of the most beautiful girl in the region," pleaded Orunmila. "She has won the hearts of all the men, but I want her only for myself. I want her for my wife."

"And what do you need me for?" asked Elegua.

"Only you, Elegua, who is such a wily trickster, can find out the secret of her name."

Elegua smiled modestly. "I'll try," he said.

He went directly to Oshun's mother's house. He stayed there for days. Some days, he disguised himself as an old man. Other days, he maintained his surveillance in the aspect of a small child. He spent days acting the fool in the local markets, hoping that a loose word would reveal the secret. Or, he pretended to be asleep in Oshun's doorway, the better to hear what went on inside.

Patience always has its rewards. After many days of patient waiting, Elegua, dozing in the doorway, heard an argument inside.

Oshun's mother, who was always very careful never to say her daughter's name aloud, was very angry. Oshun had knocked over a fresh pot of Omiero while trying out a new and exciting dance step.

"Oshun, look what you've done!" shouted the mother.

Elegua heard. "Oshun, Oshun," he said to himself. "That Oshun is going to cost you a daughter, dear lady. That Oshun will turn a daughter into a wife."

Elegua didn't waste any time in getting back to Orunmila's house.

"Well?" asked Orunmila anxiously.

"This has not been easy," said Elegua.

"What have you found out?"

"I had to spend weeks in the most uncomfortable positions," said Elegua.

"What is her name?"

"Weeks and weeks I spent wearing itchy beards and a small boy's body," said Elegua. "I'm all cramped."

"Please?" pleaded Orunmila.

"Her name is Oshun."

Orunmila ran to Oshun's house. He knocked on the door, and she opened it.

"You are going to be my wife because now I know your name," he told her.

"What is this? What is this?" asked the mother, appearing behind Oshun.

"Your name is Oshun," said Orunmila, pointing his finger at her. "And now you are mine."

The two of them were married and were happy for some time but. . . .

Men kept making offers and improper advances to Oshun, even now that she was a married woman. She paid no attention to any of them.

One day, at a party, she glanced at the drummer, who was able to pull heavenly rhythms out of his instrument. Oshun was smitten. She was transfixed by love. She kept looking at the handsome drummer and saying to herself, "He will be mine." The miraculous drummer was none other than Chango.

"Chango, do you see her?" asked the other Orishas at the party. "Oshun, the most beautiful of all, is trying to flirt with you."

"So?" asked Chango, concentrating on an especially difficult passage.

"Make love to her," said the Orishas. "She is beautiful and wants you."

Chango smiled at his friends and replied, "I have more women than I know what to do with. They throw themselves at me."

"Braggart," thought the other Orishas.

"Besides," said Chango, counterpointing his decision with the beat of the drums. "I'm not ready for any more complications right now."

That was what Chango said, but who can resist Oshun's enchantments? Who can say no to her grace and her flirtatious ways? Who can let her walk away after seeing her hips swaying? Who can refuse the invitation of her moist, fleshy lips?

Chango, the great womanizer, the great conqueror, could not resist. He became interested in her. Oshun, for her part, became colder as Chango grew warmer. She wanted to teach him a lesson for having slighted her on their first meeting.

It became too much for Chango. He waited for Orunmila to leave his house one day, went to the door, and knocked. When Oshun answered, Chango burst in.

"If you don't give me your love," said Chango, grabbing her arms, "I'll go off to war and never return."

Oshun's heart melted. "Don't go," she said. "I'll love you forever."

"Forever?" asked Chango, a little taken aback.

"I'll be with you all your life," said Oshun. "I'll be your wife."

On that day, she left Orunmila's house and went to live with Chango. Their love produced the Ibeyi.

Notes: Oshun is the most beautiful Orisha. She is sexy, flirtatious, and happy. As goddess of rivers, she loves to bathe naked in natural springs.

As Chango's wife, she is understanding of the difficulties in love and marriage. She also helps those with money problems, since she controls the purse strings in Chango's household. But the petitioner should beware: Oshun can take money away as easily as she bestows it.

Oshun loves parties and celebrations. No one has ever seen her cry. When Oshun takes over the body of a believer during a "golpe de Santo," she laughs continuously and puts on the airs of a distinguished society lady. Her arrival is always greeted with the words *"yeye dari yeyeo."*

CHAPTER SIX

The Gods (cont.)

Oya (Yansan)

SAINT: OUR LADY OF THE PRESENTATION OF OUR LORD (SANTA VIRGEN de la Candelaria) and St. Theresa.

Day of the Week: Wednesday. Friday is also popular.

Colors and Collars (Ilekes): Black and white. The collar is made up of nine black beads followed by nine white beads. Then a black bead alternates with a white bead nine times. The pattern is repeated to the desired length. A variant is a collar made of brown beads striped in a variety of colors or lilac or maroon beads striped with colors.

Sacrificial Animals: Chickens and guinea hens. Some hold that Oya does not eat any four-legged animals, but others say that she likes female goats.

Sacrificial Foods: *Ekru-Aro* (black-eyed peas unpeeled and cooked in a double boiler). Her favorite fruit is the star apple. Oya loves eggplant. All of her food should be liberally laced with corojo butter. She drinks chequete. Her water should be rain water.

Herbs: Peppercress, marigold, plantain, Jamaican rosewood, mimosa, mugwort, aralia, camphor, breakax, cypress, flamboyan tree.

Ornaments: Oya wears a crown with nine points from which hang nine charms: a hoe, a pick, a gourd, a lightning bolt, a scythe, a shovel, a rake, an ax, and a mattock. A spear or a metal rendition of a lightning bolt. A red gourd. The dried seed pod of the flamboyan tree. She also wears nine copper bracelets.

Apataki: Many years ago, Chango was embroiled in one of his unending wars. He had fought for many days and killed many of his enemies, but more came than he could kill. He found himself surrounded by them in the middle of the forest.

"Echinle," he shouted, but his famous magical horse had become lost during the fighting. Chango was afraid to yell again. He might be found.

He heard his enemies beating the bushes and shaking the trees to find him. If they did, they would kill him.

Without Echinle, Chango had to scurry through gullies and cover himself in river mud to hide from his enemies. Days passed. His implacable opponents did not rest. They did not eat. Chango, tired and hurt, had to keep on running without sleep and without food.

He ran and he ran until he reached the place where Oya lived. It was very deep in the woods. Very few people there knew that Oya was Chango's wife.

Chango came to Oya's house and pounded on the door. She opened it and saw him bruised, cut, and panting.

"What has happened to you?" cried Oya.

"Oya, they have me surrounded," panted Chango. "They want to hang me from a tree."

"Come in, quickly," said Oya, hustling Chango into her house.

"My lightning is not effective against my enemies today," he told Oya.

"That's because you lack the courage to fight," she scolded. Oya gave him water and a bite to eat.

"It's not courage I lack," said Chango. "I'm very tired."

"What do you want from me?" asked Oya.

"If I could escape my enemies' deadly circle, I could rest and sleep," said Chango. "I would recover my strength and destroy them."

"Why is it that you only come to see me when you need help?" asked Oya.

In those ancient times, Chango was used to fighting by himself, but he swallowed his pride.

"Help me, Oya."

Oya thought for a moment and then turned to her husband.

"When night falls," she said. "You will put on one of my dresses. The disguise will let you escape."

"They will still recognize my face," said Chango.

"I will cut off my hair and put it on your head. That will complete the disguise," said Oya. "I will cut off my hair to save my king's life."

They waited until night. Oya lit no fire. She was afraid that the smoke from her chimney would be noticed by Chango's enemies and draw them to the house.

When the sun had gone down, but before the moon had risen, Oya cut off her beautiful hair and pinned it to Chango's head. Chango did not know what to do with a woman's hair. It fell across his eyes. It tangled in his ears. Oya had him sit down and wove the hair into two long braids.

"Here's a dress," she said. "Put it on quickly, before the moon comes up."

Chango managed to tangle himself up in Oya's dress. "Stand still," she said. "Just stand still and let me dress you."

Finally, Chango was dressed as a passable imitation of Oya. She went to the door and peered out.

"Hurry," she said. "There's no one around."

Chango stepped outside, imitating Oya's dignified walk. He walked until he reached the forest and came across the line of searching men. He greeted his enemies with an imperious tilt of his head and crossed their line. He did not speak to them because his voice is very deep. It would have given him away. This is the way Chango was able to escape his enemies' trap.

Once he was far away from the forest, he made camp. He rested and slept and ate and regained his strength and his will to fight.

Echinle managed to find his way back to his master. Chango fed and groomed him. A few days later, rested and healed, Chango mounted Echinle.

"It is time to kill," said Chango to his horse and galloped off to find his enemies.

It was dawn when he reached his enemies' camp. He came rushing at them. His fury was terrible to behold. Lightning flashed from his hands. He shouted wild warrior cries. He was still dressed as a woman.

"Oya has turned into Chango," his enemies shouted when they saw the screaming apparition bearing down upon them, long hair flying and a gown flapping in the wind. They panicked.

Behind them, Oya, fully armed, came striding out of her house and began hacking right and left with her ax. Her short hair bristled and shot out electric sparks.

"If Oya helps Chango, there is victory," she shouted, cutting off arms and legs.

Chango and Oya were victorious. Since that battle, Oya has been Chango's inseparable companion in war. With Chango's thunder and Oya's storms, they are invincible and remain so to this day.

Notes: Oya is the only Orisha who has power over the dead. Since she is a compassionate Orisha, she has allowed many dying children to live as a gift to their parents. Cemeteries are known as *"ile yansan,"* Oya's house. Anyone who uses dead bodies or parts of dead bodies in their ceremonies must render payment and homage to Oya.

Whenever there is a haunting, Oya is summoned to dismiss the spirit. Sacrifices must be made to ensure that she takes an interest in the matter.

Oya is the Orisha of tornadoes and twisting storms, hurricanes and gales. The four winds are dominated by Elegua, Orunmila, Obatala, and Oya.

Oya has such a terrible face that anyone looking on it will be stricken mad or blind. In ceremonies where Oya descends, no one looks upon her. When she possesses someone, she puts on a red crepe dress or a flowered dress and weaves multicolored ribbons around her head. She only dances warrior dances. When her "children" enter trance, some of them can handle live coals with their bare hands.

Yemaya (Olocum, Ocute)

Saint: Our Lady of Regla (La Virgen de Regla). The patron Saint of Havana's port.

Day of the Week: Friday. Saturday is also popular.

Colors and Collars (Ilekes): White or crystal and blue. The collar is made up of seven crystal beads followed by seven blue beads. Then a crystal bead alternates with a blue bead seven times. The sequence is repeated until the desired length is obtained.

Sacrificial Animals: Lamb, ducks, roosters, turtles, goats. Fish and pigeons.

Sacrificial Foods: Banana chips and pork cracklings washed down with chequete. Black-eyed peas. All her food should be liberally spread with sugar cane molasses. Yemaya's favorite fruit is the watermelon. Her water is sea water.

Herbs: Yellow mombin, indigo, anamu (garlic herb native to Cuba), water hyacinth, seaweed, purple basil, green pepper, chayote fruit, Bermuda grass, Florida grass, sponges, coralline, majagua, linden, salt water rushes.

Ornaments: Yemaya is summoned at the seashore with a gourd rattle. She always has a fan made of duck feathers. She owns an anchor, a key, a sun, a half moon, a siren which she holds in her open arms. It holds in its hands a ray, the head of a shovel, a conch shell, and a sea shell. All her ornaments are made of lead.

Apataki: Chango first saw the light of day thanks to Obatala (in a female aspect). However, Obatala soon became indignant with her son's pranks and threw him out of her house. Yemaya took pity on the young Orisha and raised Chango as if he were her own child.

Chango grew up and left home to find his fortune. Chango forgot the details of his upbringing. He had no past. Without roots and without goals, he wandered the world. Many years passed and many women crossed his path. He had many amorous adventures. So many, that he forgot, in time, Yemaya's face.

Time passed. Chango kept chasing women, fighting, and going to parties. It was at one of these parties that Chango met Yemaya again. He was drumming and singing. The people were dancing. When he looked up, he saw Yemaya.

He immediately felt a very strong attraction toward her. His heart opened, and he felt an intense tenderness wash over him. He did not remember feeling like that before; so, he confused it with passion and sexual attraction. He was wrong. What he felt was the love of a son for his mother, his second mother, the woman who had brought him up.

He stopped playing the drums, stood up, and sidled up to Yemaya. "Have I met you somewhere before?" he asked.

Yemaya turned her back on him for an answer.

"We could go off and be alone," said Chango. "Just you and I."

His lips brushed her shoulder. She shrugged him off.

Yemaya knew the dissolute life that Chango had been leading. She knew he was a drinker, a brawler, and a womanizer. When he attempted to seduce her, his own mother, she decided to teach him a lesson.

"I'm going to teach him respect for women," she said to herself. "I'm also going to teach him a little humility." She turned to Chango. "What did you have in mind?"

Chango jumped at the opening. "Let's go to your house and keep this party going. But more privately." He did not want to go to his house, since his wives would not exactly approve of a conquest under their own roof.

"Why, I think that's a wonderful idea," purred Yemaya, leading him on. "Come with me."

She walked through the crowd. Chango was close behind.

"What an easy conquest," he said to himself. "What a virile man am I."

They walked through the sleeping town until they came to the seashore. Yemaya went to a small boat tied to a rock and got in the boat.

"Please undo the lines," she told Chango.

"But where is your house?" asked Chango. "I thought that you wanted to have a little party."

"My house is over there," said Yemaya, pointing toward the dark line of the horizon. "Come with me."

She stretched out her hand to Chango, who gingerly climbed into the boat. He was rapidly losing his enthusiasm for this romantic adventure. He was afraid of boats and did not like the water because he could not swim. But it was too late to change his mind. He would appear frightened. He was, but he would not admit it to any man, let alone a woman.

Chango tightened his grip on the gunwale as the little boat bobbed over the breakers and headed out to sea. The farther out they went, the more nervous Chango became. The little boat was out of sight of land.

"That's enough," said Chango.

"Isn't the sky lovely?" said Yemaya.

"I said, that's enough," growled Chango, striking the oars from her hands. "Who are you who has the strength to send this boat flying over the waves?"

Yemaya did not answer. She sat in the boat calmly, her hands crossed on her lap.

"Who are you who can live out in the middle of the ocean?" demanded Chango.

Instead of answering him, Yemaya dove over the side and swam straight down to the bottom of the sea.

Chango was petrified. He had no idea how to handle a boat. He didn't know what to do. Clumsily, he picked up an oar, but got it tangled in the lines coiled in the bottom of the boat.

While Chango struggled, Yemaya sent a gigantic wave toward him. It was a wave taller than a mountain. When he saw the wave coming, Chango dropped the oars and covered his head with his hands.

"I can triumph over men," he muttered, curled up in the bottom of the boat. "I can triumph over women. But I can't triumph over this wave." He took a peek over the side. A blue wall of water was bearing down upon him. He tried to make himself small. He tried to make himself disappear.

The giant wave came crashing down on him. It washed him off the boat and sent him tumbling and bubbling to the bottom of the sea. It was quiet and blue. Chango was afraid.

He fought his way back to the surface and felt immensely grateful to Olodumare when he was able to pull in a lungful of air. The boat was floating right next to him. He scrambled into it. He had not sunk and drowned. Yemaya came gliding on the waves, her feet barely touching the water.

"I think you are going to have to save me," said Chango through chattering teeth.

"I will save you upon one condition," said Yemaya.

"Name your condition."

"You must respect your mother," said Yemaya.

"My mother!" blustered Chango. "My mother abandoned me when I was a baby."

At that instant, Obatala, Chango's mother, who had been magically aware of the lesson being given to her son by Yemaya, appeared in the boat.

"You have to respect Yemaya," said Obatala. "She is your mother."

"You are my mother," he yelled. "You abandoned me when I was a child. You kicked me out of your house."

"I brought you into the world," said Obatala. "But it was up to another to bring you up."

"You forget women too easily, Chango," said Yemaya. "You have hated your mother, but you have forgotten your second mother."

"You have forgotten that she is your mother, as well as I," said Obatala. "I brought you into this world and she raised you."

"You have two mothers, Chango," said Yemaya. "You have two mothers in a world where many people have none."

A stiff breeze sprang up and washed Chango clean of the hatred he had carried for many years.

"I'm sorry," he said. "I'm sorry I hated you, Obatala. I'm sorry I forgot you, Yemaya." He sighed. "It is indeed wonderful to have two mothers."

From that time on, he began to respect women more. But he is still a womanizer.

Notes: Yemaya is the Orisha who controls all the seas and the oceans and all the creatures that live in them. She is considered the mother of all human beings.

When Yemaya comes down and possesses someone, she endows him or her with all her grace and very spicy personality. She will immediately call for a long gown tightly belted at the waist and for her fan. She dances with movements that are like the movement of the waves. When the drums heat up, she dances like waves in a hurricane.

She is full of love and tenderness, as befits the mother of all mankind.

Babalu-Aye (Chopono, Taita Cañeme)

Saint: St. Lazarus.

Day of the Week: Sunday. Wednesday is also popular.

Colors and Collars (Ilekes): White with blue streaks. The collar is made up of white beads with blue streaks strung out to the desired length.

Sacrificial Animals: Gelded goat, spotted rooster. Also, chickens, guinea hens, snakes, quail, and wild pigs.

Sacrificial Foods: Fermented corn meal. Babalu-Aye loves to drink aguardiente and to smoke good cigars. Coconut butter (ori) is his favorite condiment. His water should come from a pond.

Babalu-Aye has simple tastes and will accept, with a piece of stale bread and a glass of milk or water, dry wine and a few peanuts if the petitioner cannot afford anything better.

Herbs: Guava, balsam apple, thistles, all types of beans and seeds, peanuts, guaguasi (loetia apelata: tree native to Cuba), Virginia creeper, pigeon peas, agave, heliotrope, caroba, bastard feverfew, basil, sage, pine nut, caisimon (pothomorphe peltata L. Mig.: medicinal plant native to Cuba), yaya lancewood, cowhage, broom, rose of Jericho, datura, cocillana bark, sabicu, olive, sesame, cactus pear, and butterfly jasmine, among others.

Ornaments: Babalu-Aye always has his crutches and his two faithful little dogs. On his altar there is always a charara, a broom made from the fruit clusters of the palmetto, used to sweep away evil influences. Jute sacks also belong to him. Devotees who have been cured due to his intervention wear clothing made from jute in gratitude.

Apataki: A long time ago, Olodumare, the Supreme Being, the Creator of all the Orishas, decided to give his children a gift. He called them all together.

"My children," he told them. "It is time for you to take over your responsibilities in this world."

There were a few polite coughs. There were also a few giggles.

"I have decided to share my powers with you," continued Olodumare, after staring down the gigglers. "I will give you of my Ashé so that you may fulfill your destinies as best you are able."

All the Orishas got very excited. This was the big moment when their influence among mankind was going to be determined. They shuffled and sorted themselves out in a line.

"Oshun," said Olodumare. "To you I give the rivers."

"Thank you, Father," said Oshun.

"Chango, to you I give thunder."

"Thank you, Father," said Chango.

"Oya, to you I give the wind and the shooting stars," said Olodumare. "To you, Ogun, I give all the metals of the earth. Orunmila, I give you the power of divination so that you may guide the destiny of mankind. Elegua, Elegua, quit talking and listen to me! Elegua, to you I entrust all paths, ways, and entrances, and, since you love to talk so much, I'll make you the messenger of the Orishas."

Then came Babalu-Aye's turn.

"Is there a particular boon you would like me to bestow upon you, Babalu-Aye?" asked Olodumare.

Back then, Babalu-Aye was very good looking and very young. His primary concern was his ability to make love to women, as many of them as he could.

"I want you to give me the power to be every woman's lover," said Babalu-Aye. "I want to dally with the ladies. I want them to love me."

Olodumare frowned at such a frivolous request. "It is granted," he said. "But I want you to have one condition so that you may still have to exercise some control over your desires. On every Thursday of Easter Week, you are forbidden to have contact with a woman."

"Thank you, Father," said Babalu-Aye. "I will do as you say."

For a long time, Babalu-Aye respected Olodumare's prohibition. Every Easter Week, he would go into his house and stay away from women. But one day, on an Easter Week, he was working on his garden. He looked up and saw the most beautiful woman he had ever seen.

"Hello," he said. "Would you like to see my beautiful garden?"

Every day he talked to her. Then he held her hand. Then, on Ash Wednesday, they kissed. She came by on Thursday, and Babalu-Aye touched her, kissed her, and took her to his bed.

The next morning, when he woke up, he found his whole body covered with large, painful sores.

"What is wrong with you?" screamed the young lady, leaping out of bed.

"It's Olodumare's punishment." Babalu-Aye was afraid. "It's his punishment because I did not follow his law."

"You're disgusting," cried the young lady, and she ran out of the house.

For many days, Babalu-Aye stayed home and tried herbal baths, prayers, and sacrifices. Nothing worked. Leprosy was consuming his body. Finally he dragged himself on his stumps to Olodumare's house and knocked at the door.

"What is that smell?" said Olodumare as he opened the door.

"It is I, Babalu-Aye. I need your help."

"I seem to remember someone by that name," said Olodumare. "But he was young and handsome and knew how to keep his promises."

"Please, Olodumare," begged Babalu-Aye. "Please help me. I'm sorry I broke your commandment."

"I'm sorry," said Olodumare. "But I don't speak to people who do not keep their word."

He slammed the door on Babalu-Aye's face. And, right there, on the street in front of Olodumare's house, Babalu-Aye died with horrible convulsions and sufferings.

Babalu-Aye's death was mourned by all the women in the world. They decided to send a petition to Oshun, the Orisha of love. The women were graciously received at Oshun's house.

"What may I do for you?" asked Oshun.

"Dearest Lady, we ask you to bring Babalu-Aye back to life," they cried. "The women of the world are saddened at the horrible death of one who loved them so."

Oshun was moved by their prayers. "Ladies," she said. "I will go to Olodumare's house and try to bring your lover back to you."

That evening, Oshun went to Olodumare's house. She found a side door open and went in without anyone's seeing her. She went from room to room, sprinkling her *oñi* everywhere. Oshun's oñi is her power to awaken uncontrollable passion in men.

Olodumare, sitting quietly and reading the paper, began to shift and wiggle. He threw the paper down and ran to his wardrobe closet. He felt great and he wanted to look great. He put on his best clothes and put perfumed pomade on what was left of his hair. He thought about old lovers whom he had not seen in years and wondered what had become of them. All the passions that had lain dormant for ages of the world awoke. He looked at himself in the mirror.

"I haven't felt this good in a very long time. I haven't thought about sex in an even longer time," he said to himself.

Wise as he is, Olodumare knew that he was under the spell of Oshun's oñi.

"Oshun," he laughed. "Are you in here?"

"Here I am, Olodumare."

"Thank you," he said. "Thank you for making me feel wonderful."

"You see," said Oshun. "It's not such a bad thing to feel good. You punished Babalu-Aye for this very thing."

"Give me some more of your oñi," said Olodumare. "I feel young again."

"Only if you forgive Babalu-Aye's indiscretion," said Oshun. "If you bring him back to life, I will give you my oñi."

Olodumare had already decided to revive Babalu-Aye, since he had considered his death a temporary punishment anyway.

"Granted," said Olodumare. "Babalu-Aye will live again."

Oshun gave her oñi to Olodumare, and Olodumare gave life to Babalu-Aye. But Babalu-Aye's sores never went away.

Notes: In his African guise of Chopono, Babalu-Aye brought smallpox and leprosy to the tribes, but now he cures. His cures are always miraculous, especially among persons who are unable to walk. Babalu-Aye is full of compassion toward human suffering and misery. He knows more about pain than any of the other Orishas.

When he takes over the body of a believer, the trance is characterized by muscle cramps. The individual walks with difficulty and, at times, rolls on the floor, feeling all of Babalu-Aye's sores burning into his skin. If the pain gets to be too much for the person possessed, the head and feet are sprinkled with water.

CHAPTER SEVEN

The Gods (cont.)

Ogun

SAINT: ST. PETER. SOMETIMES OGUN IS ALSO REPRESENTED AS THE ARCH-angel Michael.

Day of the Week: Tuesday.

Colors and Collars (Ilekes): Green and black. Seven green beads followed by seven black beads. Then, a green bead alternates with a black bead seven times. The pattern is repeated until the desired length is obtained.

Sacrificial Animals: Young bulls, roosters (especially white and red roosters). All other quadrupeds.

Sacrificial Foods: Smoked fish and smoked jutia. Yam with blood. The sapodilla is his favorite fruit. All his food should be heavily smeared with corojo butter. Ogun drinks aguardiente. His water should come from a standing pond.

Herbs: Eucalyptus, sarsparilla, boneset, blessed thistle, restharrow, senna, datura, carpenter ants, guao (*comocladia dentada*: tree native to Cuba), sweet soursop, guamao (*lonchocarpus sericeus*: Cuban timber tree), red pepper, black pepper, mastic tree, castor oil plant, oak leaves, and indigo plant among others.

Ornaments: Ogun's clothing is a tiger skin. He owns an iron pot on three stubby legs and nine or twenty-one pieces of iron that symbolize all the tools used in agriculture and blacksmithing. The most common tools are an arrow, an anvil, a pickaxe, a hatchet, a machete, a hammer, and a key. Ogun's tools are always well greased with corojo butter.

Apataki: For as long as anyone can remember, for as long as there is memory, Ogun and Chango have been enemies. The way it is told by some, their hatred goes back to their childhoods.

It is said that Ogun had sex with his mother. The incestuous relationship took the mother's affections away from the father. Chango,

65

Ogun's younger brother, grew up and found out about his brother's illicit love. He decided to take vengeance.

Ogun and Oya were lovers. Chango waited and watched Ogun's house until he saw that he left Oya alone. He went to the door and, being a strong and fierce warrior, had no difficulty knocking it down.

He went in, grabbed Oya, and ignored her protests.

"You are coming with me now," he told her. "You are going to be my woman."

When Ogun returned, he searched the house for Oya. The neighbors told him what had happened. Furious, Ogun ran to Chango's house.

Chango had made love to Oya. His sexual prowess had made her fall madly in love with him.

Ogun hammered on Chango's door. Chango stuck his head out a window.

"What do you want?" shouted Chango.

"I want my woman back," yelled Ogun.

"Well, let's see if she wants to go back with you," said Chango.

Oya leaned out the window.

"What do you want, little man?" she shouted. "Go back home. I'm quite happy here."

Ogun's face got very red. His throat swelled like a bull's.

"He has put a spell on you," he shouted. "I don't care if he is the god of thunder. I'm going to make you mine again and destroy him."

Oya's and Chango's laughter was his answer. Ogun and Chango have been mortal enemies ever since.

That's one version, but another story tells of the time when Ogun and Chango met each other in the forest.

When he saw Chango, Ogun pounded his chest. "Chango, I challenge you." He drove his huge spear into the earth between Chango's legs. "We haven't fought each other in a long time. It's time to show you that I'm the better warrior," bragged Ogun.

"When do you want to fight?" asked Chango without raising his voice.

"I want to fight right now!" roared Ogun.

"I agree with you," said Chango. "I want to fight you right now too."

With a yell, Ogun grabbed his spear and rushed at Chango.

"Wait, wait," said Chango. "Let's not rush matters. We have the rest of our lives in which to fight each other. Let's do this right."

"What do you mean?" growled Ogun.

"Let's have a drink first," said Chango. "Aren't you thirsty?" And he took a large gulp from his gourd full of aguardiente.

"Let me have some," said Ogun. "Watching you drink makes me thirsty."

Chango handed him the gourd. "Have a good drink of aguardiente. I'll wait. We have all day to fight."

Chango knew that Ogun loved strong drink. He also knew that Ogun had no capacity for alcohol. After just a couple of gulps from the gourd, Ogun was weaving and laughing at nothing.

Ogun had two or three more slugs from the gourd. They went right to his head. His eyes got very red; so did his nose and ears.

"I'm ready to fight now," he yelled at Chango. "Get ready. I'm going to destroy you."

Of course, Ogun could do nothing of the kind, since he was now blind drunk. He whirled his arms, trying to hit Chango. Chango picked him up and threw him on the ground. Ogun tried to get up, but Chango jumped up and down on his chest, picked him up by his feet, and swung his head against a tree. Ogun's head made a very unpleasant sound as it hit the tree trunk.

Chango left Ogun lying on the ground. The ants went into Ogun's nose and into his ears.

An hour later, Ogun came to. His head hurt terribly. His whole body was covered with insect bites, and, what's worse, he felt like a complete fool for allowing Chango to play a dirty trick on him. He got to his feet slowly, blowing the ants out of his nose. He held on to the tree trunk for support.

"I will never forgive you," he croaked, shaking his fist in the direction of Chango's house. "I will never forgive this."

And he didn't. Ogun never forgave Chango. They have been enemies ever since.

Notes: Ogun rules all the metals. He is the only Orisha who can handle iron. All the trades that use metal tools, from the butcher to the steel worker to the surgeon, are protected by Ogun. He protects all warriors. Anyone wanting to work with a knife, a sword, or an ax has to sacrifice to Ogun.

Ogun disguises himself in order to observe his "children." He can appear as a laborer, a hunter, or a warrior. He also likes to dress up as a butcher or a smith. His wrath is terrible and usually takes the form of a bloody accident.

When Ogun comes down and possesses a Santero or Santera, he dances vigorous warrior dances and pretends to be clearing a path through the forest so that his warriors can follow him. Chango and Ogun should never be summoned in the same ceremony. If they gain possession of bodies at the same time, the two "caballos" will try to fight to the death, no matter how holy the occasion.

Osain

Saint: St. John (San Jose) in the city and St. Ambrose in the countryside.

Day of the Week: Sunday.

Colors and Collars (Ilekes): White, red, and yellow. The collar is made up of one white bead followed by nine red beads and eight yellow beads. The pattern is repeated until the desired length is obtained.

Sacrificial Animals: Goats and red roosters, turtles, turkeys, guinea hens, quail, black male doves, owls, monkeys. All reptiles, especially the crocodile. Osain will receive the feathers and the blood of pheasants, the heart of mockingbirds, and the feathers and blood of hummingbirds. He also likes peacock feathers.

Sacrificial Foods: The sap of trees and herbs. Seeds, flowers, and grains. Tobacco. He often appears to people with insomnia and asks them for a light. He drinks aguardiente.

Herbs: All medicinal and magical herbs belong to Osain.

Ornaments: Osain is never without his pipe. His Otanes and cowrie shells are kept in a gourd. The drums used in Santeria ceremonies are consecrated to him.

Apataki: As his knowledge of herbal magic grew, Osain thought himself to be Orunmila's superior. Envy made his thoughts black.

"If I get rid of Orunmila," he muttered to himself, "I will have his powers and gifts as well as my own. I will be the most powerful Orisha."

Osain began to cast powerful spells against Orunmila. All Orunmila knew was that spells and evil influences were weaving a black web around his person. He began to have slight accidents, and his health began to suffer. He attempted to use his oracular powers to find out who wished him harm, but Osain had been very careful to hide the source of his attack. Finally, Orunmila went to Chango's house.

"You must help me, Chango," said Orunmila. "My powers are not enough to see who is trying to harm me."

"I will join my vision to yours, and we're sure to discover who your enemy is," said Chango.

Chango is a great diviner in his own right. He is not as gifted as Orunmila, but, when he added his sight to Orunmila's, a wall opened and they both saw Osain's face. Not only that, they saw Osain busily brewing his spells against Orunmila.

Chango was furious. He gathered his warrior aspects around himself.

"Don't worry any more. I will rid you of that evil Orisha who is out to harm you," said Chango.

He stalked off to find Osain. First, he stopped off at Oya's house, since he brought her along whenever he prepared for war. He explained the situation to her.

"I not only want to punish him," he told her. "I want to take all his powers and knowledge away."

"I agree. We have to make him harmless," said Oya.

"Not only that," said Chango. "We will then have all his knowledge to ourselves."

Oya walks faster than Chango. She arrived at Osain's house first. She knocked at his door.

"What do you want?" asked Osain. A great cloud of herbal vapors swirled around him.

"I was just passing by and I saw all the smoke," said Oya. "I want to offer you a little aguardiente, since you seem to be working so hard."

Osain took the gourd from her hands and took a good long drink.

"Thank you, Oya," he said. "But now I have to keep working."

"Have another little drink," she said, offering her gourd again. "It's not good to work all day."

"That's true. It affects the health." Osain took another drink.

The aguardiente was already having an effect on him; so he didn't say anything when Oya walked into his house.

"I think I'll have another little drink," said Osain.

"Drink up. I have plenty," said Oya.

Osain drank and drank until he had to lie down. He fell asleep. Oya put her hands on his head and began to take his secrets. But she had underestimated Osain's capacity for drink. He woke up and grabbed her wrists.

"So, that's why you came," he shouted. "You wanted to steal my secrets."

Oya broke away and ran out into the garden with Osain close behind her.

"You can't get away. I'm going to kill you," he shouted.

He leaped and landed on Oya's back. Oya bit and clawed him. They rolled over and over among the herbs.

"Chango! Chango, help me!" screamed Oya.

Chango heard her screams. He ran around the house and jumped over the garden wall.

"You are brave enough to fight a woman," yelled Chango. "Let's see if you are brave enough to fight a warrior."

He threw a thunderbolt that tore off Osain's left arm. Holding the spurting stump, Osain ran back to his cauldrons and grabbed a gourd that held his most potent and dangerous magical herbs. Before he could throw it, Chango let loose with another thunderbolt meant to strike Osain blind. Osain ducked his head just in time, and it only tore off his ear, leaving a little nub. The pain made him drop the gourd, which shattered on the ground.

"I'm going to take chunks off you until there is nothing left," growled Chango.

He would have whittled Osain down to nothing, but he only got to strike him a couple of times. As Chango was winding up more thunderbolts, Ogun, that terrible warrior and Chango's sworn enemy, appeared. Ogun changed himself into a lightning rod and prevented any more thunderbolts from reaching Osain.

Since that fight, Osain has been a small shriveled Orisha. He only has one arm and one leg and a very small nub of an ear. He gets around by giving little hops, like a bird.

Notes: In Santeria, each plant has its own Ashé, its magical power, which can be either harmful or beneficial. Osain knows them all. Cultivated food plants hold no interest for him.

The Babalawos and Iyalochas who serve Osain are great herbalists. They follow an oral tradition which describes the properties of thousands of plants.

The Babalawo or Iyalocha must refrain from sex the night before going out to gather herbs. Once deep in the woods, he or she leaves as payment to Osain an offering of aguardiente and a little package with tobacco and a few coins.

When a plant is going to be used, the necessary offerings must be made to Osain to ensure the effectiveness of the herb's Ashé.

Osain never possesses anyone at a "golpe de Santo."

Oshosi

Saint: St. Norbert.

Day of the Week: Tuesday.

Colors and Collars (Ilekes): Green. The collar is made up of green beads. Brown and green are also popular.

Sacrificial Animals: Deer, red roosters. Sheep, goat, pigs.

Sacrificial Foods: Smoked fish and smoked jutia. Yams. Mango is his favorite fruit. All his food should be liberally covered with corojo butter. He drinks aguardiente. Oshosi's water should come from a well.

Herbs: Leadwort, esparto grass, fulminate, incense, tobacco, vine arbor, Jamaican rosewood, castor oil plant, and basil among others.

Ornaments: A bow and arrow. A model of a jail.

Apataki: Before becoming an Orisha, Oshosi earned his livelihood and supported his mother by his skills as a hunter. He knew every nook and cranny of the forest. He knew all the habits of the animals. One day, as Oshosi was walking along a forest path, Orunmila appeared to him.

"Oshosi, hear me," said Orunmila.

"I am yours to command," said Oshosi, bowing low.

"Please stand up," said Orunmila. "I am here to ask for your help."

"It is not for me to help an Orisha," said Oshosi. "But I will do what I can."

"I have need of your skills as a hunter. Olodumare wants one of the fat, delicious quail found in this area. I promised I would get him one, but I have been here for three days and haven't had any luck," confessed Orunmila. "I just don't know how to hunt them."

"Why, that would be no trouble at all," said Oshosi.

"If you get one of those quail for me, you will have my and Olodumare's blessing for the rest of your life," said Orunmila.

"Meet me at my house tomorrow," said Oshosi. "I will have a quail for you."

Orunmila disappeared. Oshosi immediately set about hunting quail. With his skill and knowledge, it wasn't very long before he had a beautiful hen struggling inside his sack. Whistling, he made his way back home.

Oshosi put the quail hen in a little cage and went back into the woods to hunt. He traveled a long way and, as was his custom, spent the night under a tree.

The following morning, he hurried home to meet Orunmila. Visions of all the wonderful things he would ask Olodumare made his head spin. His mother would be so happy!

Orunmila was already waiting when Oshosi arrived home.

"Good morning, Oshosi. Were you able to trap a quail?" Orunmila asked him.

"I trapped the fattest and most beautiful quail in all the forest," said Oshosi.

He went in the house. He came out with an empty cage.

"Where is it?" asked Orunmila.

"I don't understand it," said Oshosi. "I left it in this cage yesterday afternoon, and now it is gone."

"Are you playing with me?" Orunmila was becoming angry.

"Of course not, sir. I would not dare," said Oshosi. "Mother!"

Drying her wrinkled hands, Oshosi's little mother came out of the house.

"Yes, my son?"

"Mother, do you know anything about the quail I left in this cage yesterday afternoon?"

"No, dear," she said. "I don't know anything."

Oshosi's mother was lying. She had seen the quail in its cage the day before. She had been happy that her thoughtful son had brought her such a tasty bird to eat. She had killed, plucked, and eaten it, but she was afraid of admitting this to Orunmila.

"Don't worry, Orunmila. I will go out right now, and I will have another beautiful bird for you by this afternoon," said Oshosi.

It was not hard to keep his promise. In just one hour, he had another beautiful quail hen struggling inside his sack. He returned to his house. Orunmila was waiting for him.

72

"You see," said Oshosi, proudly taking the fluttering quail out of the sack. "I have brought you another beautiful quail."

"You have done me such a great favor that I will take you directly to Olodumare so you can present him with this quail yourself," said Orunmila. "It is not just that I should receive the credit when it was your skill that made Olodumare's gift possible."

They went to Olodumare's house. He was delighted with the quail.

"You have made my heart glad today," said Olodumare.

"It is my pleasure to honor you, great sir," responded Oshosi.

"I thank you too, Orunmila, for having had the wisdom to turn over your task to this great hunter," said Olodumare. "I have decided to make you an Orisha, Oshosi. You will be a king among hunters."

Praise and treasures were heaped on Oshosi. He did not let it go to his head but kept a pleasing humility before Olodumare. After all the ceremonies were over, Oshosi approached Olodumare.

"Sir, I would ask that you grant me one more boon," said Oshosi.

"And what might that be?" asked Olodumare.

"I have not forgiven the one who stole the first quail that I trapped for you," said Oshosi. "I want vengeance. Please allow that, when I release my arrow, it will find the thief's heart."

"I cannot deny you what you wish," said Olodumare sadly. "But you will not forgive yourself for asking such a boon."

Oshosi released his arrow, and, guided by Olodumare's will, it went straight into Oshosi's mother's breast. Horrified, Oshosi watched his mother die by his own hand. After the funeral, Oshosi stood before Olodumare, tears streaming down his cheeks.

"I will no longer be a hunter. I will fulfill my duty and help all hunters, but I will never forget that it was my need for vengeance and my lack of foresight that caused my mother's death."

Notes: Oshosi lives in the forests and is a close friend of Osain's. Osain has revealed many herbal secrets to him.

Oshosi often battles alongside Elegua and Ogun. Together, they form an invincible combination.

When Oshosi comes down during a "golpe de Santo" and possesses a believer, the person always pretends to be shooting with a bow and arrow.

Orishaoco

Saint: St. Ysidro (St. Isidro).

Day of the Week: Sunday.

Colors and Collars (Ilekes): Lilac. His collar is made up of lilac beads.

Sacrificial Animals: Red roosters, monkeys.

Sacrificial Foods: Yams and all produce from the garden.

Herbs: Yam, sweet potato, datura, bejuco colorado (*serjania diversifolia*), and everything that grows in a garden and is cultivated.

Ornaments: A hoe and all the tools of the gardener.

Notes: Orishaoco is in charge of crops and agriculture. He settles fights among the Orishas and always acts as a judge in delicate cases. He spends a lot of time resolving the arguments between Chango and his wives.

During full moon, the women whose task it is to do the gardening make offerings to him. The majority of his followers are women, and it is mostly Iyalochas who serve at his ceremonies.

The Ibeyi (Taebo and Kainde)

Saint: St. Cosme and St. Damian.

Day of the Week: Sunday.

Colors and Collars (Ilekes): The colors and collars are the same as Oshun's and Chango's, the Ibeyi's parents.

Sacrificial Animals: Pigs, sheep, goats, bull calves, and donkeys. Men who suffer from impotency or other sexual problems only offer the testicles of these animals.

Sacrificial Foods: Candies and sweets.

Herbs: Palm, gourds, coco plum, corn, gemip, sago palm, sapodilla, tomato.

Ornaments: The Ibeyi should always be dressed identically. Their figurines should be tied or chained together to insure that they won't separate.

Apataki: Obatala was known among the other Orishas for his generosity. His thrifty habits assured him of having enough money to

74

help anyone who needed help. Unfortunately, word spread that he kept money in his house.

He was robbed many times. He tried putting his money under the bed. He tried putting his money on the roof. He buried his money in the yard. No luck. Every time he found a new hiding place for his money, thieves would break in while he was taking a message to Olodumare. Obatala always came home to an empty house.

He could not stand it any more. Obatala was too noble to resent the robberies, but he was tired of having his floors dug up and his walls caved in by industrious thieves. He went to Oshosi.

"Make me the longest ladder in the world and a big strong sack," he told Oshosi.

When Oshosi had finished working and brought him the ladder and the sack, Obatala went to his house and filled the big sack with money. He then went to the middle of the forest, he found the tallest tree in the world, and used his ladder to climb to the top. There Obatala hung his money bag.

The Ibeyi had seen everything. They ran to find Chango.

"Chango, Chango! We know where Obatala's money is," they shouted. "We saw him hide it at the top of a tree!"

This news made Chango very happy. His drunken parties had been financed many times by Obatala's money. He now had the chance to get the month's drinking money. Chango was proud of his boys.

"Show me where it is," he told them. And they set off for the forest.

Chango and the Ibeyi found the tree, but Obatala had surrounded it with fierce wild animals that attacked anyone who came close. Chango thought and thought and came up with an idea.

"Give me your candy," he told the Ibeyi. "When we get the money, I will buy you twice as much."

"Make it three times as much," said the greedy twins, "and it's a deal." Chango agreed, and the Ibeyi gave him all their candies and pastries.

Chango spread the food around the tree and, while the wild animals were busy eating it, climbed to the top and dropped the bag with Obatala's money down to the twins. Chango was not seen for a month. The Ibeyi had a feast.

Notes: The Ibeyi are identical twins who represent fortune, good luck, and prosperity. In all the ceremonies, their images are always tied together to prevent their separation. If they do separate, all of their power to bring good luck disappears. They are practical jokers like Elegua, but, unlike him, they never injure anyone.

They do not come down during ceremonies to possess anyone, but dancers dance for their pleasure and honor by imitating the little hops and skips that very small children make while playing.

CHAPTER EIGHT

The Oracles

THE ORACLES ARE USED TO OBTAIN THE ORISHAS' OPINIONS AND ADVICE, to see into the future, to counsel those who come to a Santero to seek help, and to see what will heal the sick.

The most popular oracles used in Santeria are the coconut oracle (El Coco or Biague) and the cowrie shell oracle (Los Caracoles or Dilogun).

The Coconuts (El Coco, Biague)

The coconut oracle is known as Biague to honor the name of the first Babalawo to make use of Olodumare's gift. According to an old African tale, Olodumare came to earth and became so enchanted by a coconut palm that he decided to give it a gift.

"Not only will you give nourishment and oil to men," said Olodumare to the palm. "But all the Orishas will read the future in you. The pieces of your fruit will have meaning to the Orishas. They in turn will pass it on to men."

The oracle operates by interpreting the positions that four pieces of coconut shell (the *Obinu*) land in when thrown. The Obinu always respond yes or no; so questions to the Biague must be very direct and to the point. For example, the question "Should I change my job?" may have any of the following answers: ALAFIA: Yes. It is possible; EYIFE: Yes. Definitely; OTAWE: Not sure. Throw again; OCANASODE: No; OYEKUN: Death. Stop consulting the oracle and go to a Babalawo to find out what's going on. The simpler the question, the easier the answer's interpretation.

The Obinu are simply pieces of a coconut shell. What gives them their oracular power is the Ashé, the Santero or Santera's grace and natural psychic gifts. It is the Ashé which allows the consultant's relationship with the Orishas. Not everyone can use the Biague.

When one consults the Biague, questions should only be asked of one Orisha at a time. If the person consulting the oracle is not experienced in its manipulation or interpretation, only Elegua should be invoked.

The Biague may be consulted daily, but the same question should not be repeated. Elegua will become bored and play tricks on the questioner. Strange and very upsetting answers will come up. Stupid questions insult the Orishas. The oracle is not to be used as a party game or as an amusement. The Orishas are helpful when treated with respect, but they punish disrespect.

Persons who have not been initiated into Santeria, or do not have an Elegua, may consult the Biague as long as they show proper respect toward the Orishas. The prayers and invocations to Elegua may be made in the person's own language and in his or her own words.

HOW TO CONSULT THE BIAGUE

Have two gourds standing by, one filled with fresh river water (water from a faucet is not considered as effective) and one filled with the following mixture: a pinch of toasted corn; a pinch of smoked jutia (if smoked jutia is unavailable, as it is likely to be, it may be replaced by smoked fish); a smear of corojo butter; a spoonful of molasses or honey; a spoonful of powdered eggshell.

Also have a candle ready. The candle should be of a color pleasing to the Orisha being consulted. For example, if Elegua is invoked, the candle should be red and black.

Strip the outer husk off a coconut until the inner nut is freed. Take the nut in one hand and split it apart by hitting it with a hard object. A hammer will do. Tap around the nut's circumference until it splits open. Note that the inside of the nut is full of coconut milk, which will pour out when the nut is split open.

If you are inside, do not throw the coconut against the floor to open it. It is considered disrespectful to the Orishas. However, the coconut may be taken outside and split open by throwing it against a rock or a cement patio floor.

After you split the coconut apart, choose four clean pieces. They must not show any cracks or other imperfections. These will be the Obinu. Wash them in the gourd filled with fresh river water.

Take up the Obinu in your left hand. With your right hand pick out bits of coconut meat from the corners of each piece. The number of pinches should correspond to a number pleasing to the Orisha consulted. For example, pinch out three pieces for Elegua, six pieces for Chango, five pieces for Oshun, or seven pieces for Yemaya.

As you are pinching out the pieces of coconut meat, chant: *obinú ikú obinú ano obinú eyo obinú ofó arikú babagwá.* Save the pieces.

Light a candle in honor of the Orisha being consulted. Assuming that Elegua is the Orisha whose advice you seek, the candle may be placed before the image of Elegua or, if you do not have an Elegua, by the front door.

Take the small pieces of coconut you pinched off the Obinu and place them on top of Elegua's tureen or on a small plate next to the candle. Take up the gourd with the *Saraceo* mixture and add leaves of witch hazel, sargasso, or neat's tongue to it. Add enough river water to make a thick gruel. Place the gourd next to the candle and the coconut meat as an offering to Elegua.

Sprinkle river water three times around the offering while chanting *omi tutu ana tutu tutu laroye tutu ilé.* Take the gourd full of Saraceo mixture and spill a little bit in each corner of the room. Throw a few drops out the front door to guard against an unfavorable oracle. This cleansing will also help you change an unfavorable oracle should one still come up.

Once the cleansing of the room is completed, offer this prayer to Elegua: *elegua laroye akiloye aguro tente onú apagurá akama sesé areletuse abamula omubatá okoloofofó okoloñiñi toni kan ofó omoró ogun oyona alayiki agó.* You may also compose a prayer of your own, in your own language.

Other Orishas may be invoked by using one of the following prayers, or, again, you may compose your own.

MOYUBAS TO THE ORISHAS

To Elegua: *laroye akiloye aguro tente onú apagurá akama sesé areletuse abamula omubatá okóloofofó okoloñiñi toni kan ofó omoró agun oyona alayiki agó.*

To Ogun: *Ogun ñakobié kobú kobú alaguere ogúo ogun yumu su ogun finamalú egueleyein andaloro ekum feyú tana guaraguru osibiriki alalúo agó.*

To Oshosi: *oshosi odematá onibebé ede kuresé olebure atamasile eobeki agó.*

To Obatala: *obatalá obataisa obatayanu obirigwalano katioke okuni ayé kofiedenu babámi ayaguná leyibó jekun babá odumila oduaremu asabi olodo babámi ayuba.*

To Chango: *eluwekon ashé osain cherere adashé kokoni jikoji omó la dufetini cherebinu oluosó bogwó ayalu kosó agó.*

To Yemaya: *yemayá aguayo a kere odun a limí karabio osa ñabio legu eyin tebié gwá sirueku yebwá obini duato okuba okana kwana keku yanza ori eré gwá mio agó.*

To Oshun: *Yeiyé kari imbamoro ofi kereme ogwá meri kokuasi agó.*

To Osain: *osain ake meyi oshe kure kere meyi bero eki dibi agwanakero ama te le iku mori chase le berike a yaya agó.*

To Orunmila: *orunmila egwadoni en agwaluri ñakiedé ifá omá ifá ogwó ifá arikú babagwá agó.*

To Babalu-Aye: *babalú ayé ogoro niga iba elobi agwa litala babá sinlao iba eloni ogoro niga chapkuaná agó.*

To the Ibeyi: *beyi oro araba aina kainde ideu agó.*

To Orishaoco: *orishaoko ikú afefé orogodó gailotigwaro agó.*

To Biague and Adiototo (the first Babalawo to use the oracle and his son): *oshé bile adagwe biagué babadona orun adiatoto adafum ala kenta dada omo tuyo agó.*

After the Orisha who is to answer through the Biague is summoned, respect is paid to the following entities: Olodumare—*bogwo ikú oluwo embesesé olodumare ayuba igbaé bayé tonú;* the dead Santeros and Babalawos—*boguo imaworo iyalosha babalosha babalao olorisha iku embelese ibae bayeral baye tonu;* and the spirits of the dead—*kosi ikú kosi ano kosi eyo kosi ofó arikú babagwá.* Ask your Godmother and your Godfather for permission to throw the Biague, even though they may not be present: *kinkamashe* (your Godmother), kinkamashe (your Godfather).

Gather the Obinu in your right hand even if you are left-handed. Without kneeling, touch the floor and the Orisha's tureen with your left hand and say: *ilé mókueo* [the Orisha's name] *mó kueo.* Repeat the words three times. If anyone else is present, he or she should respond: *akué yé*. Place your right hand over your heart and say: *unile ovi elegua*. Bend down and moisten the fingers of your left hand in the water that you spilled on the floor. Moisten your right hand with the wet fingers and say: *akué yé oguó akué yé omá arikú babagwá*. If anyone is present, he or she should respond: *apkuaná*. Toss the Obinu on the floor while saying *oni elé bake*. If you are consulting the Biague on behalf of another person, touch the Obinu to his or her head before throwing them.

Now that you have followed the preliminary steps, the position of the Obinu on the floor determines the answer. The possible permutations are as follows.

Alafia

Chango and Orunmila speak.
Position: All four Obinu land white (meat) side up.
Meaning: Affirmative. It is possible.
Interpretation: Happiness and health. Everything has been done as is right and proper. Peace, prosperity, and grace.
Further action: When Alafia comes up, say, *eyionlé obatalá orú ayé*. Then, lie down on the floor before the Obinu and make reverence to them. Repeat the question and throw the Obinu again. Alafia must be ratified by Otawe or Eyife.

Eyife

Elegua, Ogun, Oshosi, and Oshun speak.
Position: Two Obinu white side up. Two dark side up.
Meaning: Yes.
Interpretation: Absolutely positive. Definitely affirmative.
Further action: When Eyife comes up, say, *eyífe olówo eyité omó arikú babao arikú babagwá*. If the previous throw was Alafia, the answer is yes. No need to throw again.

Otawe

Chango, Ogun, Yemaya, and Oshosi speak.

Position: Three Obinu land white side up. One lands dark (shell) side up.

Meaning: Maybe. There are doubts.

Interpretation: Hope, but not complete confidence. What is asked is possible but subject to conditions.

Further action: When Otawe comes up, say, *obara ni bara obara koso telerio ayé kikaté ala kamake arayé eluwekon ashé osain ogun arere la boko.* The Obinu must be thrown again. This time, make your question more specific. The next throw will give the answer. If Otawe comes up again, the answer is no.

With Otawe, or if the previous throw was Alafia, it might be necessary to make Ebo, a sacrifice. By consulting the oracle, the type of sacrifice can be pinpointed.

Ocanasode

Chango, Babalu-Aye, and the spirits of the dead speak.

Position: One Obinu white side up. The other three pieces are dark side up.

Meaning: No.

Interpretation: Negative. Beware of tragedy. Be alert in order to avoid misfortune. Grave difficulty.

Further action: When Ocanasode comes up, open your eyes wide, pull your ears, and say, *ocana sode okuá ti sode sode oke sode oma sode oguó batiosode arikú babagwá.* Consult the oracle again and ask if Ocanasode just means "No" or if there are further difficulties and complications present.

Oyekun

Chango and Oya speak.
Position: All four Obinu are dark side up.
Meaning: Death.
Interpretation: Definitely no. A very bad sign which announces death and suffering.
Further action: When Oyekun comes up, take the four Obinu and put them in a gourd filled with water and eight pieces of cocoa butter. This will refresh the Obinu from such a negative reading. After the Obinu are soaking in water, touch your chest and say: *olufina*. Touch the floor and say: *mofin karé mofin karé godo godo da fá mofin karé godo ba é alafi kisieko beké lorié eña kan ori mi aferé asaka beke ouani moyuba abe ebami oma tun oma ese erbami che fun ni omó omó ni mi yegwá jekua jeri apú yan fú yanzaará orún.*

A Babalawo must be consulted immediately. You need to be ritually cleansed by a *despojo,* the brushing and washing away of evil influences. Light a candle for the souls of the dead.

The Babalawo and you must keep asking the oracle if the message of death comes from the Orishas who speak or from the spirits of the dead. That will give the Babalawo an idea of the forces he must deal with.

CHAPTER NINE

The Oracles (cont.)

The Cowrie Shells (Los Caracoles, Dilogun)

THE COWRIE SHELLS, *LOS CARACOLES,* "TALK" THROUGH THE NATURAL opening of the shell. Before you can use them for divination, you must file the domed side of the shells flat until you have made a hollow shell medallion. Leave the side with the opening in its natural state.

A "hand" of shells is made up of eighteen cowrie shells. Set two of the shells aside and do not file them down. They are known as the *Edele* and become the guardians of the oracle. To the sixteen remaining shells, add a small black stone and a piece of eggshell, which will be used in manipulating the oracle, and a small bone which proves that the cowries have drunk blood (see the section on the initiation ceremony).

The person consulting the oracle holds the little black stone in one hand and the piece of eggshell in the other. According to whether the *Ordun,* the "letter," thrown is left- or right-handed, the Santero manipulating the oracle asks the questioner for the item held in that hand. If it is the black stone, the Ordun's meaning is negative. If it is the piece of eggshell, the Ordun's meaning is positive.

An unfavorable reading is an *Osobo.* The Ordun comes down "a bad path," and the negative aspects of the reading are to be stressed. A favorable reading is known as an *Iré.* The Ordun comes down "a good path," and the positive aspects of the reading are to be stressed.

The Ordun are divided and placed as follows:

Division of the Ordun
The Lesser Ordun: 5, 6, 7, 9, and 11.
The Greater Ordun: 1, 2, 3, 4, 8, 10, 12, 13, 14, 15, and 16.

Placement of the Ordun
Left hand:

All the greater Ordun. All double numbers and 6–7, 6–9, 6–5, 11–9, 9–7, 9–5, 7–5, 1–5, 3–7, 8–9, 10–6, 12–6, 11–5, 10–11, 2–6, 4–11, 1–2, 11–6, 2–5, 1–4, 1–6.

Right hand:

All the lesser Ordun and 5–9, 11–3, 5–12, 5–6, 6–12, 7–6, 11–1, 9–12, 5–11, 5–7, 11–10.

During the development of the oracle reading, the greater Ordun are thrown once and the lesser Ordun are thrown two times. The throw is repeated after a lesser Ordun comes up. However, the first throw is always repeated, regardless of whether a major or a minor Ordun comes up.

HOW TO CONSULT THE DILOGUN

The person consulting the oracle and the Santero operating the cowrie shells should sit on a mat on the floor. Both should be in their bare feet. The shells are washed in Omiero and receive a blood offering.

The Santero will then ask the questioner to write his or her name and date of birth on a small piece of paper. It is placed in the blood.

A Moyuba is made to the Orishas, Olodumare, and the spirits of the dead using the same formulas as for consulting the Biague. After the Moyuba, the Santero says: *sunsorobi baofó unsorofóbaobi.*

The Santero picks up the handful of shells and blows into them to give them his Ashé. He then puts them before the questioner's mouth so that he or she may blow on them as well.

The cowrie shells are tossed on the mat. The Santero counts the number of shells that fall with their natural openings facing up. This number determines the Ordun, the "letter." The Santero then interprets the meaning of the Ordun according to his or her experience, knowledge, and Ashé.

The first Ordun is read. It will always be made up of two numbers, since the first throw is always repeated. The dominant hand of the throw is determined, and the black stone or the eggshell will be revealed, determining whether the Ordun brings good or evil.

Ebos, prayers and sacrifices, are made to the Orishas who speak through the Ordun. If the initial throws indicate that the general answer to the question is positive, Iré, the oracle is questioned to narrow down the answer.

The first question should be *eboda?* Is it beneficial? Does it bode well for the questioner? The second question should be *ire ariku?* Are the spirits of the dead, the Iku, favorably disposed toward the questioner? The third question should be *ire ariku moyale?* Is their favorable disposition good and firm?

When the answers to these three questions are affirmative, it's clear that the questioner's path is free of any obstacles. It is only necessary to perform the Ebo according to the Ordun's instructions. The questioner will then be certain of the announced good fortune.

If a negative response is received to any or all of the previous questions, a more extensive Ebo is required to obtain a better Ordun or to improve the reading of the Ordun that have already come up.

If the first Ordun are negative, Osobo, another series of questions should be made to avoid, or at least determine, the extent of the coming misfortune. The first question should be *ocha kuaribó?* Is the misfortune sent by the Orishas? If the answer is no, ask: *egún kuaribó?* Is the misfortune sent by the dead? Once the source of the misfortune is determined, ask: *lariche?* Are the Orishas going to speak about the impending misfortune? If the answer is no, ask: *adimu?* Should a small offering be made to pacify an Orisha? If the answer is no, ask: *ebochure?* Is an Ebo of a little bit of all the Orisha's foods required? If the answer is no, ask: *enoqueun eduqueun?* Do the Orishas or spirits want something to eat today and then something to eat tomorrow? If the answer is no, ask: *ebo?* Do the Orishas want sacrifices or prayers other than those already indicated by the Ordun?

If they will accept an Ebo, then it's necessary to ask what they want and how they want it. If the answer to that is no, the Orishas do not want anything to do with the questioner and they desire nothing from him or her.

You should only consult the Dilogun once a month.

Of the sixteen Ordun that can be formed by the cowrie shells' fall, only twelve can be read by a Santero. Numbers thirteen, fourteen, fifteen, and sixteen can only be deciphered by a Babalawo.

However, there is a common interpretation of number sixteen which is "MEDILOGUN: You already belong to an Orisha whether you know it or not. You are a 'child' of Olodumare. You will be taught the science of *Ifa*. You will study the arts of healing, and, because of your learning, you will act within Santeria as a teacher and a judge for Olodumare." It is imperative that anyone receiving this Ordun consult a Babalawo immediately.

If all the cowrie shells land with their openings down, a zero, throw water up into the air so that it falls down like rain. If this happens during a double throw, interpret the single number that comes up by itself.

The Ordun

1. OCANA SODE (ONE OPENING UP)

Elegua, Chango, Obatala, and the spirits of the dead speak.

Oracle: *Ocanshosho Ofotele Obitele*—With one, the world began. If there is no good, there is no evil.

Interpretation: Pay attention and listen well to what you are about to hear.

If there is no sickness in your house now, there soon will be. Most likely, an elderly person, not you. Summon the doctor immediately. The sickness will be serious, a matter of life or death.

Take care not to be bitten by a dog.

Don't curse yourself or your luck. Don't allow your companions and relatives to do so. This habit is attracting evil influences to you and your home.

You are being held back. You are going through bad times both economically and emotionally.

You will take a trip far from home. Beware. You may be assaulted. Make sure someone takes care of your home and belongings, since you may be robbed and lose your valuables.

Resist that urge you have to do harm. Avoid arguments. Keep your mouth shut, even if you are insulted. Do not fight.

You are moody and somewhat of a joker. This may prove harmful. If your jokes and actions shame another person, there may be serious repercussions.

Ebo: When this Ordun comes up, say, *ocana sode okuá ti sode sode oke sode oma sode oguó batiosode arikú babagwá.* Place the cowrie shells in a gourd filled with water. Rinse them well. Take out the shells and throw the water out the front door. Throw the shells on the floor.

Examine the new Ordun that comes up. Step on the shells three times with your left foot. If there is a maiden in the house, ask her to pick up the shells.

Based on the second Ordun, ask the oracle if the misfortune is on the way. As soon as the question is spoken, take a piece of red meat, smear it well with corojo butter, and touch everyone present with it. Touch their foreheads, the napes of their necks, the shoulders, the palms of their hands, and their knees. Toss the meat out the door for a stray animal to take away. This will alleviate the negative influences.

Sacrifice a chick at your front door for Elegua. Rub the blood on the door frame. Hang a bunch of bananas from the door for Chango. To one side of the door, make an offering of fresh fish, a gourd filled with corn, and a tamale.

If someone comes to spread gossip, spill water three times on the floor and drink a sip of what is left in the glass. Don't get up to investigate when you hear a fight, loud voices, or noise.

Offer the Orishas a rooster, two doves, a plantain, two tamales, honey, toasted corn, smoked fish, smoked jutia, cow's meat, two coconuts, and a yam.

DOUBLE ORDUN

1–2 *Ocashonsho Abure:* When you release arrows, release them with care. If you are careless, you might injure yourself or your best friend.

1–3 *Ocashonsho Ocana:* Your dead enemy wishes the worst for you. The dead may not be so dead.

1–4 *Eyeru:* A revolution inside your body. Hemorrhages of the mouth, the nose, and the anus.

1–5 *Oshe Iku Rono:* Jealousy is the mother of mistrust. Your jealousy destroys everything.

1–6 *Leri Leri Iku:* Don't lose your head. If you don't lose your head, you won't lose yourself. The dead walk.

1–7 *Ordi Yemaya Dubuele:* One who dreams with the dead or with the sea cannot fear either one.

1–8 *Obatala Eri Ole:* When you think that you will be robbed, shut your door tight and use your head.

1–9 *Osa Enrofeo Eque:* A fight between man and wife brings tragedy. Envy brings gossip. Divorce.

1–10 *Aseyu Afefa:* He who is overly fond of gold never has any. He who embraces a lot cannot squeeze very hard.

1–11 *Oshosi Ogure:* He who is troublesome and stubborn comes to a bad end with his bones in jail. Bad, very bad.

1–12 *Ican Ina Omi:* Don't try to put out fires with mouthfuls of water.

1–13 *Oma Metanla Ocua:* The careless leader is killed and his position usurped.

2. EYIOCO (TWO OPENINGS UP)

The Ibeyi, Oshosi, Elegua, Ogun, Obatala, and Chango speak.

Oracle: *Ofa Abure*—A fight among brothers. Today, your brother is your enemy.

Interpretation: Two brothers fight over something valuable. Your brother wants to injure you with witchcraft. Beware of your business partners. Don't take vengeance against those trying to harm you. You will triumph.

You are a hothead. You lose your patience and, at times, get so furious that you talk to yourself. Your Eleda, your guardian spirit, is trying to calm you down. Pay attention.

You are in bad economic straits. Your misfortune comes from your capricious character and your tendency not to listen to advice.

Go work in the fields. You will find money. Your situation will change radically.

You were born outside the city and will live outside the city again. You will have your own house and a large plot of land. At the very least, you will have well-being and satisfaction.

You are part of identical families and will have or have twins. The Ibeyi watch over you and guide you through life. If you are single, you will marry a twin. The marriage will produce many sons.

Look after your own interests. Relatives watch you. They hold treason in their hearts. Whoever you feed and support is talking behind your back. Keep feeding the needy. Don't worry if kindness is not returned. The Ibeyi will reward you.

You have a relic or talisman that is not properly made. It does not protect you as you think.

Avoid drafts. Your constitution is weak, even though you appear strong.

Ebo: You must make Ebo; otherwise, you will find yourself in the midst of legal problems that will not allow good luck to reach you. Take care of what you eat and drink, both at home and out.

Hunt two birds. Gather two coconuts, two eggs, corojo butter, and smoked fish. Sacrifice the birds to Ogun. If you have collars, feed them some of the food and the blood. If you do not have collars, get them immediately to avoid the tragedy between brothers.

Sacrifice a rooster and two pigeons. Paint a child's chair with the blood. Keep the chair behind your front door for seven days, sitting in it frequently for another seven days. Hang the chair from the rafters or on the wall until you feel your situation is changing.

DOUBLE ORDUN

2–1   Same as 1–2.

2–2   *Ironi:* A lying woman loses her husband. A lying man loses his wife.

2–3   *Tiyi Tiyu Egun:* Where there are arguments, there is no peace. They bring bad spirits.

2–4   *Otan Ibe Chenshen:* There is a rocky path before you. Remove what bothers you, and you will walk with ease.

2–5   *Oguo Nindiyale Caniosha:* Where there is money, tragedy arises.

2–6   *Oshacuaribo:* The Orishas bring a revolution.

2–7   *Ilile Yeon Ane:* He who eats a lot is killed by his mouth. Indigestion.

2–8   *Abure Oba:* They want to depose the king by filling him with arrows.

2–9   *Ore Gata Obini:* Your best friend wants your woman. Tragedy. Confusion and rumors within the family.

2–10   *Icoco Oguo:* He who arises early always has money in his pocket.

2–11   *Ajuani Oshosi:* Your birds die in their cage. Don't imprison your children. Arguments between father and son.

2–12   *Ebo Osha:* He who does not petition the Orishas fails in all endeavors.

2–13   *Otocu:* For each dead king, a new king.

3.   OGUNDA (THREE OPENINGS UP)

Ogun, Oshosi, Obatala, and Olodumare speak.

Oracle: *Lucumi Guila Acuin Urara Malama. Cuila Acuin*—Arguments and tragedy.

Interpretation: Sometimes, you feel a great desire to hit another person on the head. Don't use or carry a weapon: knife or firearm. You'll hurt yourself. Let Ogun be your weapon.

Avoid fights and arguments. You may be attacked and not have time to defend yourself.

Avoid dark places, especially bars. Danger follows you. Don't climb around in dangerous places. Avoid machinery. You may receive a puncture wound and fall ill if you don't beware.

Don't drink. Alcohol goes to your head and makes you lose your senses. It may eventually drive you crazy.

Take care if you have broken the law. You may be found out and imprisoned.

If you are married, don't fight with your spouse. A curse between man and wife may affect the children for many years.

Three people are struggling for the same thing you want. They feel their rights to it are superior. They all want to lead. They don't want you to stand out and take on responsibility.

Beware the one bearing gifts. Examine what is offered; it may harm instead of helping.

What you have lost you will regain soon. What will be lost will be found. Your crying will turn to laughter.

Ebo: Set up an Ogun in your house. If you have one, sacrifice a goat to him. Ogun will tell you how to protect yourself.

Make an Ebo to the Orishas of fresh fish, corojo butter, tamales, and coconuts. Sacrifice a dove and a rooster. Offer their tongues.

DOUBLE ORDUN

3–1 and 3–2   Same as 1–3 and 2–3.

3–3   *Ocumajana Laroye:* The drunk believes one thing and the bartender another. To offer a toast, one must first learn how to drink.

3–4   *Ocuni Iyu:* A single man may save his people.

3–5   *Icun Chere:* Don't pick up what you discarded. Loathing.

3–6   *Eyioroso Meyi:* Return what the visitor offers. Twins are coming to your house.

3–7   *Orunmila Oyu:* What is known is not questioned. Look at what is in front of your eyes. Guess the riddle.

3–8   *Tere Tere:* Don't kill mice. Don't kill what is in your house.

3–9   *Emu Fofo:* No flies enter a closed mouth. Don't gossip. Don't stick your nose in other people's business.

3–10   *Ananagu Eyorozunde:* If you are cursed, forgive him who curses you. He who forgives is saved. He who does not is doomed.

3–11   *Otaniyu:* A person throws a stone, and all his people have to carry the blame. Don't take on the problems of others.

3–12   *Ocan Ise:* Put your heart into what you do so it comes out well.

3–13   *Ade Omi Emu:* Water from a clean gourd does not stain the tongue.

4.   EYOROSUN (FOUR OPENINGS UP)

Chango, Yemaya, Oshosi, Orunmila, and the Ibeyi speak.

Oracle: *Acute*—No one knows what is at the bottom of the sea.

Interpretation: You have a lot of projects, but you can't decide what you are going to do with your life. This is causing you to pull money in with one hand and throw it away with the other.

You will run into an attractive business proposition. Beware what you sign. Have everything in writing to avoid misunderstandings. Don't worry and don't complain. The gods will provide.

You will be robbed, if you haven't been robbed already. Don't display your valuables. Don't hide money at home. Beware of visitors. Not everyone has good intentions.

A woman has evil thoughts and an evil tongue for all who surround her. She is quarrelsome and a snoop. Stay away from her. She wants to see you in jail. Don't listen to gossip about your loved ones.

If you are a married man, another man is making eyes at your wife. He wants to seduce her. He is creating arguments between the two of you for his amusement.

Don't tell anyone your innermost secrets. Envy and jealousy are everywhere.

You will become a Babalawo or an Iyalocha. You are Yemaya's "child." Babalu-Aye and Obatala protect you as well. You must make Ebo to avoid losing a sick relative.

Ebo: Go to the sea. Give a duck and a watermelon to Yemaya. She will set you on the path that is best for you.

Wear blue and white often. Offer two red roosters, four coconuts, smoked fish, and corojo butter to the Orishas. Don't walk through the woods. If you do, cleanse yourself with an herbal bath.

Don't eat grain or tripe. Don't suck on the heads of animals or gnaw on bones. Don't jump over ditches or over ropes. Keep your house clean and well lit. Do not hang things from the walls or rafters. If you have promised an Ebo to Babalu-Aye, pay him.

Place a chick, an arrow, a stick, three stones, unsalted lard, smoked jutia, and smoked fish in a frying pan. Wrap the frying pan in a sheet and present it to the Orishas.

DOUBLE ORDUN

4–1 to 4–3 are the same as 1–4 to 3–4.

4–4   *Levi Levi:* The son who was born strong, healthy, and straight is now crooked from lack of care.

4–5   *Iku Oshe:* The dead are out and about, looking for someone to capture. Run. Don't let the spirits of the dead chasing you catch you.

4–6   *Oloyuo Chenshen:* Cats walk along fences. Men do not. Make up your mind.

4–7   *Meye Oya Elese:* If your head does not sell you, no one can buy you. The head moves the feet. The feet take the body to the auction block. Think with your head and not with your feet.

4–8   *Leñi Aensa:* You were born to be a head and stayed a tail.

4–9   *Ofemi Eni:* Look forward and look back. Take care where you walk.

4–10   *Abuyalara Iron:* No one listens to a boaster.

4–11   *Funfun Terevi:* White is pretty. Dress in white.

4–12   *Eñicocoso Omemi Ardie:* Chickens were born to lay eggs. You were born to have sons. Don't avoid it.

4–13   *Ayagua:* The turtle walks slowly but gets to where she is going. Don't hurry so much. Things are better done slowly.

The Oracles (cont.)

The Cowrie Shells (Los Caracoles, Dilogun)

5. OSHE (FIVE OPENINGS UP)

OSHUN, OLODUMARE, ORUNMILA, AND ELEGUA SPEAK.

Oracle: *Eyevale Eye*—Blood that runs through the veins.

Interpretation: You have lost your great good luck. What you have loved has disappeared. At times, you feel like crying for no reason. Your difficulties are your best advisers. Your tongue is your luck and your disgrace.

You will be initiated into Santeria. You will "seat" your Orisha. You have participated in ceremonies. Ebos have been done for you. You are not satisfied. You think you have been cheated and fooled.

It is not true. You are a "child" of Oshun. She has been testing you. Don't search any more. You have found the house where all your problems will be resolved. Oshun will remove your anxiety. You have passed her tests. You are called to serve as a priest within Santeria. Don't say anything bad about other Santeros. They could not help you until you had drawn this Ordun.

A dead soul is asking your family for a mass. It wanders about incessantly and is asking for help. You will take a long trip, but you must do Ebo.

You are very nervous and may fall ill. It is not due to an Orisha or to a curse laid upon you. Go to a doctor for a sedative.

You have to move three times. The last house will be your home for years. There you will find happiness and good fortune.

Ebo: If you promised an Ebo to Oshun, pay it now. Offer a small goat to Oshun. She will help you get what you desire. Oshun wants you to give her a big party with lots of music. The size of the party you throw will determine the extent of Oshun's gifts to you.

Rub your hands with a bit of cocoa butter and rub them over your head from front to back. Do it frequently. It will calm your nerves. Make Ebo to the front door. Rub it with cocoa butter and drape it with white material.

Feed your Elegua with a smoked fish head and corojo butter to change your luck. Go out and buy a lottery ticket. Do an Ebo for your head.

Offer the Orishas five small fish, five chickens, five small gourds, five feathers from a parrot, and five peanuts. Clean your house five days in a row with clear water, five egg whites, and honey. Don't eat pumpkin, eggs, or reheated food.

DOUBLE ORDUN

5–1 to 5–4 are the same as 1–5 to 4–5.

5–5   *Sore Emu:* If you talk too much, you will tire out both your tongue and your companions. Don't talk so much.

5–6   *Ayalay:* Bells sound better in your own yard.

5–7   *Ire Logue:* You are free because of lack of proof. Don't push your luck. They may catch you with your fingers in the pudding.

5–8   *Buruenyele Odu Iron:* Lies bring arguments. There are disturbances in your house due to liars.

5–9   *Ashaesu Meunle:* No one knows what he has until he loses it. Take care of what is yours.

5–10   *Iku Ogunda Rono Colo Osha Coniguengue:* The dead took what the Orisha has. Don't pretend to be dead or a Saint. You are not going to like the wake or the burial.

5–11   *Aye Oshe Odbara:* If you don't know the laws under which you have to live or obey them, you will learn them in the next world.

5–12   *Olodumare Omemi Iya:* The good son has God's and his mother's blessing. Remember your mother. Respect your mother.

5–13   *Sirere Ican Ina:* Don't play with fire or you will get burnt.

6.   OBARA (SIX OPENINGS UP)

Chango, Oshun, and Elegua speak.

Oracle: *Oba Icoru*—From legends, the truth is born. The king does not lie.

Interpretation: You are very short of means. You lack everything. Your money vanishes like smoke. You are being held back. Whoever has a treasure and does not watch it will lose it.

You lie and are always caught at it. Your exaggerations confuse what is real with what is not. People have to take you as you are. You are not going to change. Beware that what you are told is not false. Beware others' lies. Control your mind and see things as they really are. Do not live in dreams and illusions.

Beware the law if you defend another from harm. When opportunity knocks, open the door. Make good use of it or, when your luck fails, don't complain that you threw opportunity away.

Drink is your worst enemy. Don't talk about what you see. You might benefit from having been the only witness. A man should listen to his wife's advice. You are Orunmila's "child."

Ebo: If you have an Orunmila, go to a Babalawo and have him suggest an Ebo. If you don't have one, receive him as soon as possible.

Light a candle to the Orishas. Offer a rooster and a little piece of the clothes you have on. Offer a garabato stick (a shepherd's crook or club), two roosters, sixteen small gourds, two chickens, red cloths, smoked fish, and corojo butter to the Orishas.

Don't help anyone lift anything off the floor. Make a blood Ebo to Oshun. Wear white clothes.

DOUBLE ORDUN

6–1 to 6–5 are the same as 1–6 to 5–6.

6–6   *Iku Orunmila Babalosha:* He who doesn't know, dies. He who knows lives. Go to Orunmila's house so he can tell you the luck that awaits you in this life.

6–7   *Aya Ibe:* Dogs have four legs but walk on one path. You can't be everywhere at once.

6–8   *Afuyalasa:* Where a trifle grows, nothing else will sprout.

6–9   *Asiguere:* You are not crazy. You pretend to be crazy. If you continue to pretend, you will become crazy.

6–10   *Abe Agutan:* Two calves do not drink at the same fountain.

6–11   *Aguada Eke:* Don't be envy's slave. Beware the envious.

6–12   *Saranda:* Your stubbornness will take you from failure to failure.

6–13   *Arube Chenshe:* He who does not listen to advice does not reach old age.

7. ODI (SEVEN OPENINGS UP)

Yemaya, Oshun, Ogun, and Elegua speak.

Oracle: *Odi Olocum*—Where the first hole was dug. Where the first burial was made.

Interpretation: You are very frightened. You toss and turn in bed without sleep. The spirits of the dead chase you in your dreams. Your nerves are overexcited. You do not have any strength. See a doctor. Don't allow further deterioration. What is nothing today will be extremely serious tomorrow.

Three persons compete for your favors. You are confused, but you will pick the third one, the last you meet. Beware of venereal disease and eye problems. Beware adultery's dangers.

Someone will come with gossip. Stay away from the complications. Don't risk giving advice, even with the best of intentions. Remember previous negative results in these situations.

Treachery between man and wife. Blood and tragedy. Don't listen to those who woo you. It will destroy your home. It is all a lie.

You dream of your enemies. Disappointments result from not following your premonitions. You have the gifts of seer and diviner. You see the future.

Ebo: Dress in light, happy colors. Avoid somber colors. Don't eat or drink in anyone's house.

Offer Elegua a gourd, a turtle, a chicken, two doves, two ears of corn, beans, and a rooster. Offer the Orishas two roosters, a large gourd, seven coconuts, and seven ears of corn. Offer the Orishas cloths of different colors, seven tamales, two gourds, and parrot feathers.

Raise a small lamb. Yemaya will improve your life according to how well it grows. You are Yemaya's "child" and must be initiated.

DOUBLE ORDUN

7–1 to 7–6 are the same as 1–7 to 6–7.

7–7   *Odigaga Odigogo:* Everyone makes sure that they do things with care so that they come out well. Two don't know how to do things properly.

7–8   *Azan:* Don't abandon your customs. Uneasiness.

7–9   *Ecugogo Meyi Agadogudo:* Two with big noses can't kiss.

7–10 *Cuacua Ofemi:* Don't be ashamed to look at yourself.

7–11 *Logue Cofagua:* Stretch out your hand as far as it will go.

7–12 *Leti:* The ear is smaller than the head, yet it does not go through it.

7–13 *Eta Elede:* See how much crackling is left after the fat is fried. Give everything time and you will win.

8. EYEUNLE (EIGHT OPENINGS UP)

Obatala and all the Orishas speak.

Oracle: *Leri Eri*—The head rules the body. Only one king rules the body.

Interpretation: You don't get the merit you deserve. It is your fault. You are too good, too noble. Help the needy, but don't be taken for a fool. Listen to your wife or parents when they express anger at the way your false friends are treating you.

Things may appear uncertain. Your life will change from this date forward. Don't let yourself be ordered about. Listen to advice and use your judgment. You have suffered much and still have to struggle on. In the end, your path will be clear.

You have a gift for business and dealing with people. Olodumare gave you this gift to use. Use it to benefit yourself and your employees. You were born to lead. Olodumare wants you to succeed.

Beware of robbers. Stay away from dark and dangerous places. A dream warning of danger is worrying you. You must make Ebo to turn it away. Don't count your dreams. They will lose their power. Your complaints attract negative influences. Don't curse yourself or desire your own death.

Honor Oshun, your elders, and your parents. Don't argue. Their advice is for your own good.

You have taken another's woman. The consequences will be serious.

Don't help anyone off the floor. He whom you help raise will help you fall. He will turn against you.

Sometimes you believe and sometimes you doubt. Don't ask for proofs. They may be too strong for you.

Ebo: You have to be initiated into Santeria immediately. Don't kill mice or any of Elegua's small animals.

You should have a piece of red cloth in your home that draws attention. If you don't have one, get one. Curtains, bedspread, or tablecloths are good. It should be seen as soon as your house is entered. Don't dress in red. If you'd like to, dress in white or in white with a little bit of red.

Don't eat corn or any grain. Don't eat white beans. Make an offering to the Orishas of two white doves, a stick of your own height, cocoa butter, two parrot feathers, cotton, and a piece of white cloth.

DOUBLE ORDUN

8–1 to 8–7 are the same as 1–8 to 7–8.

8–8   *Ore Gata Eruya:* When close friends fight, war is certain. Don't fight with your friends.

8–9   *Chango Yile Abo:* Don't repeat the evil that you once committed.

8–10   *Ise Sore Onia:* The needle carries the thread. Don't follow people who talk nonsense. You are being given bad counsel.

8–11   *Iyile Cocoaya Daguada:* He who eats too much gets sick. Leave some for others. You will not regret sharing what you have.

8–12   *Guan Mele Losi:* Wasps have fierce stings. The pain passes.

8–13   *Onuru Olodumare Mogueleti:* Kneeling, one talks with God. Get on your knees, and God will listen to you.

9.   OSA (NINE OPENINGS UP)

Oya, Obatala, Ogun, and Oshun speak.

Oracle: *Osa Canengue Eriate*—Your best friend is your worst enemy.

Interpretation: Problems between man and wife. The marriage is at an end. There is no rest in the house. Too much noise and fighting. The neighbors will call the law. This disagreeable situation is brought about by a person who looks upon the marriage with an evil eye. That person wants the end of the marriage. He or she is paying for witchcraft to destroy you. Beware if you are about to marry.

You feel a lot of anger. Don't argue with anyone. It prevents you from thinking intelligently. You fight over nothing. Calm down. If you are single, your fights with your parents are making you leave home.

Stop thinking about moving. Do it. Don't allow sick visitors to sleep over. If they die in your house, their spirits will trouble you. Consult a doctor. Beware of fire. When someone entrusts you with something, receive it in front of witnesses. You might be asked to return more than you were given.

Ebo: Make an Ebo to Ogun. His influence will control your anger. Don't visit cemeteries. Pray to Obatala. He will lift your sadness. If you have an Orisha who has not been fed, feed him or her.

Make an offering to the Orishas of two chickens, two doves, a small machete, nine gourds, nine buns, and two stones you find in your house, your patio, or right by your front door.

DOUBLE ORDUN

9–1 to 9–8 are the same as 1–9 to 8–9.

9–9 *Ocua Burere Ore:* A friend who kills a friend and a brother who kills a brother cannot be pardoned. Their crimes won't be forgotten.

9–10 *Omi Olofin Oyauro:* Rain water is God's water. Wash yourself in it.

9–11 *Tiyu Aqua:* You can't dig a hole where there's one already dug. Leave what is buried be, or you will suffer great shame.

9–12 *Oya Saranda Ayi Loda Logue:* You are a failure because you are a troublemaker. You will be put in the cemetery by your own hand.

9–13 *Otaco Eni Igui:* A hidden enemy in the house—hidden under the bed.

10. OFUN (TEN OPENINGS UP)

Obatala, Oshun, and Oya speak.

Oracle: *Ananaqui. Ofun Mafun Larobi*—Where the curse was born.

Interpretation: You are stubborn. You are lazy. What you think is easy is not. All your projects are up in the air. Your whims make you repent your actions. You don't like toil, but in this life one must struggle.

The ill person in your house should see a doctor and consult Orunmila. Contrary to appearances, your health is delicate. Go see a doctor.

Your gambling luck is gone. Someone is using witchcraft against you. Your job is in danger. Bet the number in your dreams to pay your bills, not to get rich.

Say a mass for your dead parents. Don't argue with living ones. You must be initiated into Santeria.

Ebo: Feed Oshun in a river. Feed Oya in a market.

You must make an Omiero. The questioner and the Santero

manipulating the oracle must both drink a little. Spill a bit on a piece of linen. Offer some to Elegua and some to Obatala. At night, throw the remaining mixture out into the street and shout "*Batiosode!*" three times.

Keep your house clean. Don't store bundles under your bed.

Offer the Orishas an Ebo made up of a rooster, a chicken, a horse's mane, powdered eggshell, cocoa butter, and tamales.

DOUBLE ORDUN

10–1 to 10–9 are the same as 1–10 to 9–10.

10–10   *Sirere Ile Ogue:* He who gambles loses the cash and his home.

10–11   *Guesum:* The cheap is expensive in the end.

10–12   *Ocumayama:* Drunks don't know what they are doing when they don't want to.

10–13   *Osain Esum:* He who rests under a strong tree benefits from the shadow.

11. OHUANI CHOBI (ELEVEN OPENINGS UP)

Babalu-Aye, Elegua, Oshun, and Oya speak.

Oracle: *Omi Ohuani Oshobi*—Bailing water with a basket. Ingratitude.

Interpretation: A black, evil dead soul is tormenting you and your family. It has been chasing you for years. You have to resort to stronger measures than masses to drive it away, or it will take you with it. This spirit drives away anyone who might help you. You have already had accidents. The next one could be fatal. Don't lose hope. Feed your Orisha.

Don't loiter on street corners. You may be falsely accused of a crime.

You don't listen to advice. You don't follow directions. That is why you never see the results of your Ebos.

Don't argue. Don't lose control. Let Oya and Elegua pay back those who have harmed you. Don't take vengeance against anyone, not even your worst enemy.

Don't drink. Don't go out at night. Don't open the door to anyone after you go to bed unless they identify themselves.

Ebo: Place an Elegua in your home. If you have one, feed him. Offer the Orishas a bottle of water, a bottle of aguardiente, eleven needles or sharp thorns, three pots, two roosters, and three corn meal balls. Offer the Orishas two roosters, two turtles, white thread, black thread, and a razor.

DOUBLE ORDUN

11–1 to 11–10 are the same as 1–11 to 10–11.

11–11 *Mentala Ohuanishobi:* You will see your enemy's corpse pass by your front door. Don't curse those who wish you evil. Olodumare will provide justice.

11–12 *Aguere Agadogodo:* A united family is a strong family. Unite your family.

11–13 *Aquisa:* A new broom sweeps clean.

12. EYILA CHEBORA (TWELVE OPENINGS UP)

Chango speaks.

Oracle: *Orecuami Obatacuami*—When there is a war, the warrior does not sleep.

Interpretation: Beware of fire. Stay away from the scenes of fires. Don't visit jails or hospitals.

Ask Chango for what you need. You are Chango's "child." You get what you want, but you can't keep it. That's because you don't respect Chango. You have been told that another Orisha protects you. That is not true. Beware of Ogun's "children." You have been a diviner since birth. If you are a man, you will be a Babalawo.

Your friends always betray your trust. They take advantage of you and gossip behind your back. Have few, but well-chosen friends. Keep your private affairs private.

You have a bad temper. Don't use or carry weapons.

Ebo: Wash your head with hog plums. Dress in white and pray to Obatala. Don't practice any sorcery involving the souls of the dead.

Make an offer to the Orishas of okra, a tiger's skin, smoked fish, smoked jutia, cocoa butter, black-eyed peas, a small club, a piece of rope, red cloth, and white cloth. Sacrifice two roosters.

DOUBLE ORDUN

12–1 to 12–11 are the same as 1–12 to 11–12.

12–12 *Egue Sarandere Sarayeyeo:* Cleanse yourself. Forward movement.

12–13   *Maferefun Orunmila:* Olodumare made Orunmila into a seer.
Your destiny is known by Orunmila.

13.   METANLA (THIRTEEN OPENINGS UP)

Babalu-Aye speaks.
Throat problems. Menstrual problems. Blood problems.
An impending illness will put your life in danger. Consult a competent Babalawo immediately.

The Oracles (cont.)

The Dominos

THE DOMINOS DO NOT REQUIRE THE CEREMONIES OF THE BIAGUE OR the Dilogun. Since they are a simple form of divination rather than an oracle, their interpretation does not require as much experience or finesse. They are not as respected or trusted as the formal oracles.

HOW TO CONSULT THE DOMINOS

You need a set of dominos up to a double six. Lay the dominos face down on a mat or table and mix them up.

Pick up a domino from the pile and compare it to the list of throws. After reading it, return it to the pile. Stir the dominos and repeat the process twice more.

If a piece comes up twice, it is a reaffirmation of the previous reading, but you have the right to pick a fourth piece.

Don't consult the dominos on Mondays or Fridays or more than once a month.

THE THROWS

Double Blank: A bad omen. Heartbreak and treachery. Lost love. Lost work. Lost business. Beware of accidents.

What you gained through treachery and the black arts you will keep. You will pay for it in sickness and suffering.

Perform an Ebo for Oya and Chango as soon as possible.

One/Blank: Someone will die in your house. You won't find luck. Beware your temper.

Go to a Babalawo and do what he says.

Double One: Happiness in business and love. Harmony in the home. Romance and matrimony. Triumph and security.

Two/Blank: Treachery and bad luck. Women, keep your eyes on your husband or boyfriend.

Travel. The change will be favorable.

Give Oshun a chicken, pound cake with honey, and five small coins.

Two/One: A marriage to wealth will end in early widowhood. The second marriage will last for many years.

Your spouse may fall ill and die. Guard your money. Robbery.

Get an amulet against envy.

Double Two: This month brings happiness and success in business. Good luck in everything you do.

An older man wants to harm you.

The Ibeyi suggest a long business trip. Make Ebo to them under the direction of your godmother or godfather. Your future depends on the Ibeyi.

Feed your collars. If you don't have any, throw the Dilogun and get collars and Ashé.

Three/Blank: A fight. The bad-tempered wife wants a divorce. Infidelity. Avoid gossip, bars, and darkened places.

Feed Elegua on Monday. Do Ebo with a white rooster and throw the Biague. Elegua will tell you what to do.

Three/One: Scandal. Problems with the law. Someone comes with bad news. You will solve the problem.

Following Three/Blank, it confirms your spouse's infidelity.

Elegua is playing tricks on you because you haven't fed him. If you don't have an Elegua, get one as soon as possible.

Three/Two: Love. Marriage. Business investments. Luck in gambling. The Orishas look after you. Honor and feed them.

Take care of your children. They feel abandoned and are upset with you.

Double Three: A large sum of money arrives. A good friend bears gifts. Recovery from illness. Reunion with a loved one.

Elegua guards your door.

Four/Blank: A broken heart. The marriage is off. Gossip and complications. An evil spirit is after you.

Consult Orunmila if you're pregnant. Twins or triplets. A difficult or premature birth.

Four/One: Marriage. Economic security. Prosperity. Act on your plans before the end of the month.

Four/Two: Big changes come for all aspects of your life. Transfers. Job changes.

Make Ebos of food and music to Chango and Elegua so that all comes out right.

Four/Three: Marriage for the single woman. A son for the married woman. A new wife for the bachelor. An affair and problems for the married man.

Double Four: Help from friends and acquaintances. A fun trip with good friends.

Five/Blank: Women, the man comes with bad intentions. Suffering. Public humiliation. Beware married men. Beware accidents on the job.

Make an Ebo for your head.

Five/One: Problems with your stomach. An addition to the family. Don't dig up buried things. Don't eat pumpkins.

You will lose money if you don't feed Oshun. Bathe in a river after offering it a lot of honey.

Five/Two: Obstacles in your life. Don't marry. Don't move. Don't travel. Anxiety. Illness. You sleep badly. Go see a doctor.

Don't change your normal routine. Don't allow yourself to be pushed around. Listen to advice.

You have the gift of foresight. Develop it. Be initiated into Santeria.

Five/Three: Peace and security in your business. A better job. You will get out of debt this month.

Five/Four: Love. Marriage. Lots of sons. Don't invest money this month.

Double Five: Love. You will succeed in everything you try.

Make an Ebo to the Orishas with lots of herbs.

Six/Blank: Two marriages. A divorce and another marriage.

Consult the Dilogun.

Six/One: Arguments between parents, sons, and brothers. Disagreeable news from far away.

Six/Two: You will recover from an operation. A business recovery. The marriage will recover. A messenger comes bringing good news.

Six/Three: All obstacles to love will be overcome. Security and consistency in all that you attempt.

Six/Four: A fast recovery. A marriage with money and lots of gifts. Someone wants to destroy your happiness. Don't worry. You will overcome all obstacles and succeed.

Six/Five: Persist in what you are doing. Radical change in your life. A new beginning. Your health may be affected, but not for long.

Double Six: Go see a Santero or a Babalawo. Receive the collars and learn about Santeria. You will find health and prosperity in Santeria. If a double six is drawn twice, you should become a Santero. Everything in your life depends on the Orishas and how you honor them.

The Chinese Numbers (Charada China, Chifa)

The *Chifa* is a simple numerological dream interpretation guide commonly used for betting and the purchase of lottery tickets. It does not really form part of Santeria, but it is so widely used, and the association between animals, persons, or objects and their number is so strong among the followers of Santeria, that an abbreviated list is worth including here.

1	Horse	2	Butterfly
3	Sailor	4	Cat, Mouth
5	Nun	6	Turtle
7	Snail	8	Corpse
9	Elephant	10	Big fish
11	Rooster	12	Whore
13	Peacock	14	Tiger
15	Dog	16	Bull
17	Moon	18	Small fish
19	Worm	20	House cat
21	Snake	22	Toad
23	Steam	24	Dove
25	Gem	26	Eel
27	Wasp	28	Goat
29	Mouse	30	Shrimp
31	Deer	32	Hog
33	Buzzard	34	Monkey
35	Spider	36	Pipe
37	Witch	38	Macaw
39	Rabbit	40	Priest
41	Lizard	42	Duck

43	Scorpion	44	Year
45	Shark	46	Bus
47	Bird	48	Roach
49	Drunk	50	Police
51	Soldier	52	Bicycle
53	Electric light	54	Flower
55	Crab	56	Candy
57	Bed	58	Photo
59	Crazy	60	Clown
61	Big horse	62	Marriage
63	Killer	64	Big corpse
65	Food	66	Horn
67	Stab	68	Cemetery
69	Well	70	Coconut
71	River	72	Ox
73	Suitcase	74	Kite
75	Tie	76	Dancer
77	Italian flag	78	Coffin
79	Train	80	Old doctor
81	Theater	82	Mother
83	Tragedy	84	Blood
85	Mirror	86	Scissors
87	Banana	88	Glasses
89	Torrents	90	Old man
91	Old shoe	92	Plane
93	Ring	94	Machete
95	War	96	Shoe
97	Mosquito	98	Piano
99	Saw	100	Toilet

Ileke and Ifa's Board

These are the most respected and complicated oracle systems in Santeria. While all the Orishas may speak through the Biague and the Dilogun, the Ileke and Ifa's Board are reserved exclusively to Orunmila, the Orisha of wisdom. Through him speaks Olodumare, the supreme deity.

Only Babalawos with their long years of experience and study under other Babalawos (who initiate them into the oracles' secrets) are able to use and interpret the mysteries of the Ileke and Ifa's Board.

The Ileke is made up of twelve collars. They are the same collars granted during the initiation ceremonies. Every morning, after saluting Olodumare, the Babalawo throws the collars to learn which influences will rule the day and what combinations of collars he should wear to make the most of the positive influences available and to ward off any impending evil.

Ifa's Board is made from a round or rectangular piece of wood known as the *Opon Ifá*. The images of the Orishas who control the quarters of the world are carved on each quadrant or corner of the board.

To use the board as an oracle, the Babalawo uses sixteen palmetto nuts or sixteen cowrie shells. He tosses the nuts or shells onto the board and interprets the pattern of their relative positions away from the corners and edges of the board as well as the individual position of each nut or shell. The possible combinations of Ifa's Board reach 4,096 Ordun. The encyclopedic scope of the interrelationships between Ordun and their Apatakis is beyond the scope of this volume.

CHAPTER TWELVE

Talismans, Spells, and Implorations (Ebos)

ALL RITES ARE PRECEDED BY EBOS. THE WORD EBO INCLUDES ALL TYPES of sacrifices and offerings of food, drink, and property. It also means a petition, an imploration, a supplication. The idea of purification is implicit in Ebo and includes the cleanliness, both physical and spiritual, of the person making Ebo.

The Ebo repertory is endless, ranging from the simplest—a small love gift of fruit or drink to an Orisha—to the most expensive and difficult to employ, demanding the death by fire of bulls and horses. The Orishas need food and blood. Blood increases their energies and keeps them potent, efficient, and satisfied with their worshipers. In turn, the Orishas render renewed strength and vitality to the person making, and to those participating in, a blood sacrifice.

Ebos are needed when one is being initiated into Santeria and is receiving the collars. They shield from danger, illness, and death. There are Ebos to obtain your heart's desire, to better your life, to succeed in any undertaking. They are also employed to protect you from witchcraft, to appease an Orisha's anger, to woo an Orisha's favors, and to distance yourself from the influence of the dead. They woo lovers and they also kill. All needs are met through Ebos.

Ebos for the Head (Eleda)

TO REFRESH THE HEAD (ELEDA)

Coconut water   River water or rain water   Raw milk
Rice water   Corojo butter
White juicy fruits, such as pineapples, pears, and sweet soursop
Mix all the ingredients together and wash your head as often as you

like. This is especially recommended for mild depression and anxiety and to get rid of the "blahs."

TO FEED THE HEAD (ELEDA)

Coconut   Powdered eggshell   Cocoa butter
Smoked fish and jutia for Elegua
Slugs and black-eyed peas tamales for Obatala
Two new white plates   Two candles   Cotton
A large white handkerchief

Feed Elegua and Obatala. Make a paste from the rest of the ingredients. Light the two candles and place one on the center of each plate.

The person whose Eleda is being fed should be sitting with his or her shoes off and holding on to his or her knees. The paste is placed on the plates around the burning candles. The Santero holds a plate in each hand and presents the offerings to the petitioner's forehead, shoulders, chest, the palms of the hands, the knees, and the feet while chanting: *"awe bo awe to awe omo ori yuba ba wa osiweo owe to mo re."*

The paste is then applied to the petitioner's head. While it is still wet, the cotton is applied, the head is covered by the handkerchief, and the paste is allowed to dry.

TO STRENGTHEN THE HEAD (ELEDA)

Four pairs of white doves   Powdered eggshell
Two coconuts   Cocoa butter   Smoked fish   Corn
Pepper   One pound of cotton   Two yards of white cloth

Have the petitioner sit as in feeding the Eleda. Tear off the doves' heads and allow the blood to drip onto the petitioner's head. Mix the coconut meat, cocoa butter, fish, corn, and pepper into a paste. Invoke the Orishas.

Cover the petitioner's head with the paste and the cotton. Wrap the head in the white cloth.

The doves are cooked in a new pot, and only the petitioner may eat them. During three days, the petitioner will wear the mixture and turban. He or she is to avoid the sun, not to go out, not to speak to anyone, become angry, or sleep on a bed.

TO SAVE A PERSON AT THE POINT OF DEATH

A white female calf   A large white container
Two pounds of cotton

Sacrifice the calf to Obatala. Cut off its head and place it for twenty-four hours next to the dying person's head. Pray and petition Obatala during the twenty-four hours.

The following day, feed the dying person's Eleda and follow the same procedure on the severed calf's head. After the Eleda is fed, wrap the calf's head in cotton and place it inside the white vessel.

Bury the vessel, with the head in it, in a cemetery.

TO THINK CLEARLY

Cotton   Powdered eggshell   Cocoa butter
Grated coconut   Grated yam   Coconut water
A white cloth

If you feel that you are not thinking with your accustomed clarity, make a paste with the yam and the grated coconut. Mix in the rest of the ingredients and soak up the result with the cotton. Wrap the soggy cotton in the white cloth.

Lie down and put the package on your forehead. Close your eyes for an hour. Keep the mixture moist by sprinkling it with coconut water.

TO SEE YOUR ORISHA OR ELEDA

Prop up a mirror on the floor of a very quiet and dark room. Light a candle next to it. Sit on the floor two to three feet away from the mirror. Look into the mirror for three hours, and you will see your Orisha, your Eleda, and your past lives.

Ebos for Petitioning the Orishas

TO PETITION YEMAYA

Water   Indigo dye   A candle

Fill a small tub with water. Tint the water with indigo until it is a deep blue. Place a candle on a small dish and float the dish on the water. Petition Yemaya as you light the candle.

The candle should burn for seven or fourteen days.

TO PETITION THE ORISHAS

Almond oil   Corojo oil   Iron filings   Coconut
Wine   Orange water   Peppercorns   Cocoa butter
Mercury   Red ocher

Fill a tin can with the oils and seven drops of wine and orange water, seven peppercorns, seven small bits of coconut, and a pinch of each of the solid ingredients. Place a wick in the mixture.

Go to the seashore and petition Yemaya and all the Orishas to come to your aid as you light the lamp. Next to the lamp, place a glass of water with cocoa butter and mercury.

TO PETITION YEMAYA

Indigo dye   Corojo butter   Corn meal   Fish
Salt   A cotton wick   A blue cloth

Fill a deep plate with liquefied corojo butter. Stir in the indigo until it is a deep blue. Add small amounts of corn meal, fish, and salt. Insert the wick and allow the corojo butter to solidify.

Petition Yemaya as you light the wick. Allow the lamp to burn until all the corojo butter is consumed. Wrap the remains in a blue cloth and dispose of the bundle at sea.

TO PETITION OSHUN

A large gourd   Five eggs   Honey   Oil
A sugar plum   Cotton wicks

Make small holes in the five eggs and place them inside the gourd. Fill the eggs with oil, a drop of honey, and a piece of sugar plum. Place a wick in each egg.

Light the wicks as you petition Oshun. The egg lamps should burn for five days. At the end of the fifth day, take the gourd and the burnt-out eggs and dispose of them in a river.

Ebos to Remove Curses and Evil Influences (Despojos)

TO REMOVE CURSED EGGS

Alcohol   Dry red wine   Camphor squares   Black pepper

When someone has cursed you by throwing or placing cursed eggs around your property, don't touch them. Sprinkle them with alcohol, dry red wine, and camphor squares. Set the mixture on fire and, while it burns, sprinkle it with black pepper and ask that the evil that is wished upon you returns to the person who sent it.

TO REMOVE AN ENEMY'S INFLUENCE

Six red apples   A red cloth   Banana leaves
A red rooster   Six red lianas

Go to the foot of a palm or a kapok tree. Take off all your clothes. Wipe yourself all over your body with the red cloth.

Spread it out on the ground. Proceed to rub yourself thoroughly with all the other ingredients and pile them on the cloth.

Finally, take the rooster and wipe yourself down with it. Tear off its head and let its blood drip upon the pile on the red cloth. Add the rooster's feathers to the pile and make a bundle.

Bury the bundle at the base of the tree. Don't go back to that place for a long time.

TO REMOVE THE TENDENCY TO BE ACCIDENT PRONE

A piece of black cloth   White chalk   Seven black roosters
Rose apple roots   A shark's tooth   A mule's tooth
Owl feathers   Seven candles   A large iron pot

Draw a cross with chalk on each corner of the black cloth. Line the inside of the iron pot with the black cloth.

Place the seven candles inside the pot and light them. Throw in the seven black roosters' legs, the rose apple roots, and the rest of the ingredients. Make sure that there are enough owl feathers for a good fire.

As all the ingredients burn inside the pot, ask to be relieved of your curse. When the fire burns out, take the pot full of ashes to a cemetery before midnight and bury the pot with its contents.

TO REMOVE THE INFLUENCE OF THE EVIL EYE FROM A CHILD

Sweet basil   Holy water   A white handkerchief

If you suspect that a child is sick because of someone's evil eye, put the child to bed. Pray over the child, asking for the intervention of your Orisha, Yemaya, St. Beltran, or your patron Catholic Saint. Moisten a sprig of sweet basil in the holy water and make crosses on the child's head, chest, stomach, legs, and hands. When you are finished, wrap the sweet basil in the white handkerchief and dispose of it far from the house.

TO REMOVE A NEIGHBOR'S EVIL EYE

Tie a red ribbon around a large bunch of bananas. Hang them until rotten from the roof of your house. They will absorb all your neighbor's envy.

TO FACILITATE A TRIP

If there are obstacles in the way of a business or pleasure trip, sacrifice a chick to Elegua. Take a few of the feathers and go to a railroad line. Rub the feathers over your hands and feet and leave them there along with twenty-one pieces of hard candy.

TO BETTER YOUR LIFE

A piece of flank steak   A red cloth   A piece of white cloth
Red ribbon   Corojo butter   Powdered eggshell
Dried corn   Six pieces of coconut   Six cowrie shells
Six silver coins   A red rooster

Place the steak on the red cloth. Smear it with corojo butter and powdered eggshell. Rub the steak thoroughly all over your naked body and then place it on the red cloth again.

Dress in red and white. To the steak add the corn, coconut, shells, and the coins. Place the red cloth and all that is on it on the piece of white cloth. Make a secure bundle and tie it with the ribbon.

Take the bundle to the base of a kapok tree and offer it to Chango. Before putting the package down, circle the tree six times while touching it with your right hand and praying to Chango for a better life. After the sixth turn, leave the package at the foot of the tree.

Wait six days and return to the tree. Sacrifice a red rooster and leave it where you left the package. Do not touch the tree. Never do another ceremony of any kind at that tree. Don't return for a long time.

TO FIND OUT WHO IS CURSING YOU

A white candle   A clear wine glass   Water
Coconut oil   Corojo butter

Go into a very quiet room. Place the wine glass on the floor and fill it with water, a couple of drops of coconut oil, and a tiny bit of corojo butter. Place the candle next to the glass and light it.

Shut out all other sources of light. Sit on the floor two or three feet away from the glass and invoke your Orisha, if you have one.

Look at the glass. Breathe evenly. It's all right to fall asleep, since the answer may come in a dream. The face of the person wishing you evil will appear in the glass. The process takes patience and perseverance, since you might see unrelated scenes in the glass for quite a while.

TO WARD OFF EVIL

Cooking oil   Five eggs   Cinnamon
A deep white dish

Fill the dish with cooking oil. Float the five eggs on the oil. Sprinkle them liberally with cinnamon. Insert a cotton wick in the oil and burn the lamp for five days.

TO WARD OFF THE EVIL EYE

A small gourd   Mazorquilla   Taro   Bamboo

Grind the ingredients to powder. Mix equal quantities of each powder and sift. Blow the powder into the eyes of the person giving you the evil eye.

TO PURIFY YOURSELF

Sunflowers   Yellow roses   White roses   Red roses
Pompeii cologne   Violet water   Mint oil   Coconut oil
Chamomile   Holy water   Rose water   Mint leaves

Put five sunflowers in a large container. Add five of each of the roses, a small bottle of cologne, a small bottle of violet water, five drops of mint oil, and five drops of coconut oil. Add a small bottle of rose water, five handfuls of chamomile, five handfuls of mint leaves, and five drops of holy water. Pour in about five gallons of water. Let the mixture steep for twenty-four hours.

Bathe with the mixture before going to bed. Don't dry it off.

TO PURIFY YOURSELF

Peppergrass   Vervain   Rosemary   Violets   Marigolds
Pumpkin seeds   Guinea pepper   Five river stones
Five peacock feathers   Five cinnamon sticks

Fill the tub with boiling water. Add five blossoms of all the flowers and five pumpkin seeds. Sprinkle in the pepper. Add the rest of the ingredients and stir until cool enough to submerge yourself.

TO PURIFY YOURSELF

Sea water   Watermelon seeds   Florida grass
Anamu (*petiveria alliacea:* garlic herb native to Cuba)
Purple basil   Mugwort   Witch hazel   Marjoram
Seven gallon bottles   Seven candles

Take all the ingredients to the seashore. Fill the seven bottles halfway with sea water. Add seven watermelon seeds to each bottle along with seven sprigs of each of the herbs. Submerge the bottles in the sea for seven hours.

Start bathing with the contents of the first bottle on a Saturday. Use a bottle a day until all the bottles are used up. On the seventh day, light seven candles to Yemaya.

Ebos to Curse

TO CURSE A PERSON

A candle from a funeral   Coal dust   Salt
Seventy pins

Buy the coal dust and salt at three different stores. Mix equal quantities in a plate. Set up the candle so that it burns upside down on the plate, on top of the mixture.

At midnight, strip yourself nude and light the candle. As it burns, let out all the hatred you feel toward the person you want to curse. Stick the pins in the candle as if it were the flesh of your enemy. With each pin, shout out that you wish the death and destruction of the hated person.

After the candle has burnt down, leave the plate at your enemy's doorstep.

TO CURSE A PERSON'S MATERIAL POSSESSIONS

Corn silk   Brown paper   Sand
Two twigs   A funeral candle

Obtain a candle that was used in a funeral nine days ago or keep one for nine days.

Using the corn silk and the paper, build a castle to the best of your ability. Strengthen the castle by pouring sand at each corner. Use the twigs as little flagstaffs.

At midnight, take the play castle to a trash pile. Take off all your clothes and light the candle, invoking the soul of the individual in whose funeral it was used. Set the castle on fire. Tell the dead soul that your enemy's goods should burn as the castle is burning. Continue demanding destruction and loss for your enemy until the castle is completely burnt. Leave the candle burning.

TO CURSE A PERSON

A used pot   Cow fat   Dirt from nine graves
Dirt from a cemetery entrance
Dirt from two corners of a cemetery   Mud from a tomb
Cat excrement   A dried quail's head   A dried bat's head
Iron filings   Cowhage   Charcoal   Guinea pepper
Chinese pepper   Indian pepper   Rock salt   Garlic
A shark's tooth   A dog's tooth   A cat's tooth   A beehive
Peonies   A hermit crab   A land crab   Dried okra
Nine cotton wicks

Fill the pot with cow fat. Put the pot on a fire and melt the fat. Stir in nine pinches of each of the cemetery dirts and mud. Add the dried heads, nine pinches of the excrement, the filings, the cowhage, peppers, nine pieces of salt, nine cloves of garlic, nine pinches of charcoal, and the teeth. Slowly add the pieces of the beehive so that the wax has a chance to melt and mix with the fat. Add nine peonies, the two crabs, and nine pieces of the dried okra. Insert the wicks.

Go to the cemetery at midnight and take off your clothes. Light the lamp and ask the souls of all the dead to torment and injure your enemy in every way possible. Leave the lamp burning in the cemetery.

TO KILL AN ENEMY

Nine clay pots   Dirt from nine tombs   Nine coins
Ashes   Guinea pepper   Chinese pepper   Black pepper

Aguardiente   Cooking oil   Nine wicks

Write the name of your victim on the bottom of each pot. Fill each of the pots with a handful of dirt from one of the tombs. Leave a coin at each tomb as payment for the dirt. Mix ashes in with the dirt. Add the peppers.

Pour nine spoonfuls of aguardiente in each pot. Fill each pot with cooking oil and insert a wick.

Go to the cemetery at midnight. Light the nine lamps and invoke the help of the souls of the dead to kill your enemy.

TO CURSE AN ENEMY

Linseed oil   Almond oil   Cooking oil   Balsam
Ashes   Three peppercorns

Write the name of your enemy on a piece of paper and place it at the bottom of a clay pot. Cover the paper with nine pinches of ashes, the peppercorns, and the balsam. Pour in equal parts of the oils and insert nine wicks.

At midnight, petition Oya to destroy your enemy as you light the lamp. Do this nine nights in a row.

TO CAUSE A TRAGEDY

Nine peppercorns   Nine pieces of rock salt
Dirt from a cemetery   Sulphur   Red ocher   Cat hairs
Hairs from your enemy   Nine roots of boneset
A scorpion   Cooking oil

Write your enemy's name nine times on a piece of paper. Wrap the boneset roots with the paper by winding it with cat hairs and your enemy's hairs. Place the roll at the bottom of a clay pot.

Cover the paper with the peppercorns, the salt, and nine pinches of the cemetery dirt. Add nine pinches of sulphur and of the red ocher.

Fill a frying pan with cooking oil. Fry a scorpion in the oil until it is completely dissolved. Pour the oil into the clay pot. Insert a wick.

Take the lamp to a cemetery and place it where no one will bother it. Light it and let it burn for nine days.

On the ninth day go retrieve the lamp. Go to your enemy's house and smash the clay pot on his front door.

TO CURSE YOUR ENEMY

A funeral candle   A knife

At midnight, light the candle and call your enemy's name. As you pronounce his name, make small cuts and stabs on the candle. Repeat the procedure for three consecutive days.

TO CURSE YOUR ENEMY

Four roosters   Sulphur   Chinese pepper   Black pepper
Mercury   Coconut   Dust from your enemy's footprint
Linseed oil   Cemetery dust   Buzzard feathers
Gunpowder   Sesame seeds   Star apple leaves
Dried red snapper   A kapok tree root

Cut off the roosters' heads and dry them in the sun. When dry, place them in a clay pot. Add nine grains of each pepper, three drops of mercury, three pieces of coconut, nine pinches of both dusts. Add three buzzard feathers, nine pinches of gunpowder, nine sesame seeds, three star apple leaves, three pieces of the red snapper, and three pieces of the kapok root. Add enough linseed oil to cover the mixture. Insert a wick.

Light the lamp at midnight, calling your enemy's name and cursing it. Leave the lamp burning for three days. Daily, at midnight, curse your enemy's name while standing in front of the lamp.

TO BRING YOUR ENEMY EVIL

Seven pins   A gourd

You must obtain a few drops of your enemy's urine. Wet the points of the pins in it. Stick the pins into a fresh gourd and bury it in a fire-ant pile.

TO BRING YOUR ENEMY EVIL

Dust from the tomb of an assassin's victim   India ink
Vinegar   Aguardiente   Salt   Red wine
Guinea pepper   Chinese pepper   Three needles

Nine pins   Three garlic bulbs   Snake fat   Cooking oil

Write your enemy's name with India ink on a piece of paper. Pierce the paper with the nine pins and the three needles. Place it at the bottom of a clay pot. Cover the paper with nine pinches of dust, salt, and the peppers. Add nine drops of India ink and vinegar, nine spoonfuls of aguardiente, nine spoonfuls of the snake fat, and the garlic bulbs. Cover the mixture with cooking oil and insert a wick.

Call a curse on your enemy as you light the lamp. Let it burn for nine days.

TO CURSE YOUR ENEMY'S HOUSE

River water   Sea water   Cooking oil   Seven turkey eggs
Charcoal powder   Guinea pepper   Fresh water

In a tub, mix equal quantities of the different waters and the oil. Add the whites from the turkey eggs, seven pinches of the charcoal, and the pepper. Stir everything thoroughly. Take care that none of the mixture is spilled in your house.

Fill seven bottles with the liquid and smash a bottle a day against your enemy's house for seven days in a row.

TO MAKE A MAN IMPOTENT

A scorpion   Cooking oil   Three lemons   Salt water
Aguardiente   Basil root

Fry the scorpion in the oil until it dissolves. Pour the oil into a pot. Add the juice of the lemons, three cups of salt water, seven drops of aguardiente, and the root. Insert a wick.

Light the lamp while calling out your enemy's name. Let it burn for three days. Dispose of the lamp in a virgin's grave.

TO MAKE A MAN IMPOTENT

Termites   Fire ants   A chicken gizzard   Sugar cubes
Body hair   Menstrual blood   Oil   Honey   A scorpion
Chinese pepper   Cotton balls   Semen

Fry the scorpion in oil until it dissolves. Save the oil.

Write the man's name on a piece of paper and wrap the chicken gizzard with it. Place it in a pot. Cover the paper with live termites and fire ants. Add three sugar cubes, three hairs from the man's body, and menstrual blood from three consecutive days. Pour in the oil. Stir in three spoonfuls of honey, three grains of Chinese pepper, and eight cotton balls with the man's semen on them. Insert a wick.

Light the lamp and let it burn for three days. Dispose of it in an empty grave.

TO MAKE A MAN IMPOTENT

Cotton balls   Turpentine   Poppy seeds
Balsam   Incense   Amansa guapo
Semen

Write the man's name on a piece of paper. Wrap the paper around a cotton ball with the man's semen on it.

Place the paper at the bottom of a pot. Cover it with poppy seeds, balsam, incense, and amansa guapo. Pour in enough turpentine to cover and insert a wick.

Place the lamp before your Elegua and burn it for three days. Take it to a cemetery on the third day and dispose of it in an empty grave.

TO CURSE A PERSON

Dust from the grave of a corpse with
the same name as your enemy
Human bone   A crab's shell   Cowhage

Pulverize the human bone, the shell, and the cowhage. Mix it in equal parts with the grave dust. Sprinkle the mixture at your enemy's doorstep.

TO CURSE A PERSON

An eggshell   A wasp's nest   Rock salt   Coal
Guinea pepper

Grind all the ingredients into a powder. Mix equal parts together and blow the powder into your enemy's face.

TO DESTROY HAPPINESS IN A HOME

Ashes   Goat excrement   Pig excrement   Dog excrement
Chinese pepper   Guinea pepper   Black pepper

Dry the excrements thoroughly and reduce them to a powder. Mix the powder in equal parts with the ashes and the peppers. Sift the mixture into a fine powder. Sprinkle inside the house you wish to curse.

TO DESTROY HAPPINESS IN A HOME

Blessed thistle   Chinese pepper   Guinea pepper
Cemetery dust

Toast and powder the thistle. Mix in equal parts with the other ingredients. Sift into a fine powder. Sprinkle on the door of the house you wish to curse.

TO DESTROY HAPPINESS IN A HOME

Fresh dog excrement   Fresh cat excrement   Dog whiskers
Cat eyelashes   Cat tail hairs   Dog tail hairs
Motor oil   Red ocher   Two roosters

Powder the animal hairs. Mix them with equal parts of the fresh excrement. Add a pinch of red ocher and enough motor oil to get a sticky consistency. Roll the mixture into a ball.

Make the two roosters fight and cut their heads off. Let the blood drip over the ball of excrement. Toss the ball onto the house's roof.

TO CAUSE ARGUMENTS

Female monkey excrement   Lion excrement
Dog excrement   Chicken excrement   A turtle shell
Cowhage

Dry all the excrements thoroughly, then powder them. Powder the turtle shell and the cowhage and mix in equal parts with the excrement. Sift to a fine powder and spread over the area where you wish the arguments and the tragedies to occur.

TO CAUSE ARGUMENTS

A twig from a red pepper bush   A turtle shell
Dust from a place where two men have fought
Rock salt   Guinea pepper   Cat hair   Red ants
Cowhage   Boneset   Bamboo

Reduce all the ingredients to powder and mix in equal quantities. Sprinkle over the area where you want the arguments to occur. If it is a house, sprinkle it on the doorstep.

TO CAUSE FIGHTS

A crab shell   A turtle shell   Human bones
Snake skin   Cowhage   Urine   Powdered antler
Red, white, and black pepper   Red ants   Boneset
Ironweed   Coal   A wasp's nest   Sesame seeds
Peony seeds   Cemetery dust   Wind-blown dust
Pig excrement   Goat excrement   Dog excrement

Burn the human bones and powder them. Dry and powder the excrements. Powder the rest of the ingredients and mix all in equal parts. Sift until a fine powder is obtained.

To use, set out three pieces of paper. Place a pinch of the mixture on each. Fold the papers up and place before your Elegua for three days.

On the third day, write the victim's name on a piece of paper. Burn the paper and add the ashes to the three small packages. Sprinkle this activated powder where you want the fight to take place.

TO DESTROY PEACE IN A HOME

Dust from a place where three dogs have fought
Cat's hairs   Mustard   Pepper   Rock salt
Dried okra seeds

Grind all the ingredients to powder and mix in equal parts. Sift into a fine powder. Sprinkle inside the house whose peace you want to destroy.

TO KILL AN ENEMY
WARNING: A DEADLY POISON!!!

Jimsonweed   Nightshade seeds
Lobelia juice   Arsenic

Dry the herbal components and reduce them to a powder. Mix the powders in equal quantities with the lobelia juice and let dry. Sift to a fine powder. Mix with your victim's food.

TO PRODUCE SWELLINGS IN AN ENEMY

Toad skin   Sesame seeds
Peony seeds   Nettles   Egg yolk
Guao (*comocladia dentata:* tree native to Cuba)

Toast the toad skin and powder it. Dry the egg yolk in the sun and powder it. Dry and powder the herbal components. Mix the ingredients in equal quantities. Sift into a fine powder. Take care that the mixture does not touch your skin. Sprinkle the powder on your enemy's body.

TO DRIVE AWAY UNPLEASANT PEOPLE

Honey   Ginger   Amansa guapo

On a plate, place three spoonfuls of honey, three pieces of ginger, and the amansa guapo. Place the plate in front of your Elegua and wait until it is covered with ants. Mix all the ingredients, including the ants, and smear the mixture over your mouth, petitioning Elegua to drive the person away.

TO DRIVE AWAY UNPLEASANT PEOPLE

Pumpkin leaves

Boil seven pumpkin leaves in water. Strain off and keep the water. When an unpleasant person comes to visit, throw out a bit of the water at the person's back as he or she is leaving. Repeat every time the person comes to visit. The person will stop coming.

TO DRIVE AWAY UNPLEASANT PEOPLE

A loaf of bread   An egg   Honey   India ink
Red ocher   A white cloth   A turtle shell
Corn silk   Corn

Make seven spots of red ocher on the white cloth. Place a tea cup atop the cloth.

Break the egg inside the tea cup. Pour in seven drops of honey and seven of ink. Add a few threads of corn silk and three grains of corn.

Tear off the butt end of a loaf of bread, hollow it out, and pour the mixture into it. Place the butt in a turtle shell and wrap everything up in the white cloth.

Wait until the person you dislike is leaving and throw out the bundle after him or her.

TO DRIVE AWAY UNPLEASANT PEOPLE

Ground cumin   Chinese pepper
Guinea pepper   Cowhage   Dried cat excrement
Dried dog excrement

Reduce each of the ingredients to a fine powder. Mix equal parts of the powders together. Blow this powder upon the person you want to drive away.

TO DRIVE AWAY AN UNPLEASANT PERSON

Take hairs from the head of a dog and of a cat. Toast them and pulverize them. Blow the powder on the unwanted person.

TO DRIVE AWAY AN UNPLEASANT PERSON

Ashes   Powdered eggshell   Hellebore root

Dry and powder the hellebore root. Mix in equal parts with the ashes and the powdered eggshell. Blow the powder into the face of the person you want to drive away.

TO DRIVE AWAY UNPLEASANT PEOPLE

Witch hazel   Marigold   Clover   Flakes of rust
Rock salt   Ground antler   A lizard skin   A frog skin
Coal   Human bone

Write the person's name on a piece of paper and burn it. Dry and powder the rest of the ingredients and add in equal quantities to the ashes. Blow this powder at the person's back and feet.

TO DRIVE AWAY UNPLEASANT PEOPLE

A pepper tree twig   A tamarind twig   Malanguilla
Clover   Marigold   Cowhage   Cemetery dust
Ground antler   Dried goat's excrement
Dried pig's excrement

Grind each of the ingredients into powder. Mix equal parts of the powders. Blow the powder at the person.

TO MAKE A PERSON WANDER WITHOUT A RESTING PLACE

Red pepper   White pepper   Black pepper   Rock salt
Coal   Ashes   India ink   Brick dust   Mud
Iron filings   Ground glass   An infertile hen's egg
Dust from the four corners of the person's house
A black cloth

Write the person's name on a piece of paper and burn it to ashes. Place the ashes on the black cloth. Cover the ashes with a pinch of each of the peppers and powders and a drop of India ink.

Blow out the white from the egg and place it on the pile of powder. Bundle up the black cloth and ingredients and throw it into an open grave.

TO DESTROY A MARRIAGE OR A FRIENDSHIP

Three guinea hen eggs   Cooking oil   Cowhage
Sow thistle   Boneset   Malanguilla
Abre camino *(bunchosia media)*   Ground pepper

Red ocher   Salt

In a new pot filled with the oil, boil three pinches of each of the ingredients except the eggs. Strain and save the oil.

Make small holes in the eggs and blow out the contents. Fill them with the oil. Place the eggs before Elegua for three days.

Go to the couple's house or the house of one of the friends. Throw an egg at each front corner of the house and one at the door.

TO DESTROY A MARRIAGE OR A FRIENDSHIP

A duck egg   Salt   A candle

Place the egg in a container. Cover it with salt and place it and the burning candle before your Elegua for three days.

On the third day, go to the couple's house or the house of one of the friends. Leave the egg on the front step.

TO DESTROY A MARRIAGE OR A FRIENDSHIP

India ink   Large piece of paper   An egg

Write the names of the persons to be separated on a large piece of paper. Cut the names apart and burn the paper. Cover the egg with the ashes for twenty-four hours.

Go to the couple's house or the house of one of the friends. Throw the egg against the front door.

Ebos to Drive Away Illness

TO DRIVE AWAY SICKNESS

Tie a dry corn cob behind the door with a purple ribbon.

TO DRIVE AWAY SICKNESS AND THE EVIL EYE

A peeled guava stick   Corojo butter
White, blue, red, yellow, black, green, and brown ribbons

Bend the guava stick into a shepherd's crook shape. Cover it thoroughly in corojo butter. Wind the seven ribbons around it. Place the stick behind the door.

TO PROTECT AGAINST A COLD OR FLU

During the cold and flu season, take a small jute bag and fill it with a few pieces of camphor and two or three mint leaves. Hang the bag from your neck or pin it to your underclothes.

TO ENCOURAGE RECUPERATION FROM AN ILLNESS

Bejuco de la cruz (*hippocratea volubiles, Lin.*)
A white ribbon   Cocoa butter   Cotton

Place a little bundle of bejuco de la cruz, tied with the white ribbon and smeared with cocoa butter, next to the bed or under the pillow. When the sick person recuperates, wrap the bundle in cotton and throw it away in a hospital.

TO RELIEVE STOMACH TROUBLES

Cinnamon sticks   Two chickens   Honey
Guinea pepper   Five small gourds   Fresh fish
Cinnamon oil   Cocoa butter   Five pieces of coconut
Five yellow candles   A piece of yellow cloth

Place the candles around the sick person. As you light each candle, pray to Oshun: "*oshun mori leyeo obini oro abebe oro osun oni cola-legue iyami loyasousun aye cari pa angara mama yeye guañasi egale guasi ori osha obini oro guasi aña ayuba maferefun.*"

Rub each of the ingredients on the sick person's stomach and place them on the yellow cloth. After the last item, blow out the candles, put them on the cloth, and wrap up the bundle.

Take the bundle to a river, open it, take out the candles, and light them. Sacrifice a chicken and allow the blood to drip on the bundle's contents. Offer the bundle to the river.

Sacrifice another chicken to Oshun and smear it with honey, cinnamon sticks, and chewed guinea pepper before giving it to the river.

This Ebo is normally done for women who have problems with their lower bellies. If the condition is not severe, a gourd smeared with cocoa butter will suffice for the Ebo.

TO PREVENT ILLNESS DUE TO THE EVIL EYE

A white dove   Cocoa butter   Corojo butter

Put cocoa butter and corojo butter on the dove's legs, wings, and head. Rub your head with the dove.

Free the dove outside your house, preferably outside your neighborhood. This Ebo should be done during the last days of the year.

Ebos to Prevent Arguments and Problems with the Law

TO SETTLE DISSENSION AT HOME AND AT WORK

Sprinkle toasted corn mixed with powdered eggshell around the area several days in a row.

TO PREVENT GOSSIP AND SLANDER

Ginger root   A cowrie shell   A young chick
A red rooster   A piece of goat skin

Sacrifice the chick and the rooster and let their blood flow over the ginger root and the shell. Make a small bag out of the goat skin. Place the root and the shell inside, still wet with blood. Add the rooster's tongue. Close up the bag and wear it close to your body.

TO PREVENT PROBLEMS WITH THE LAW

Put a white rabbit and a white dove together in a comfortable cage. Feed them well every day and sprinkle drops of holy water and coconut water on their heads.

The day before the court date, free the animals in a field. Tell them that you fed them to give them their liberty, so they should give you your freedom.

TO COOL OFF A BAD TEMPER

A lodestone   Poplar slivers   Amansa guapo
Cocillana bark   Eggshell   Cocoa butter   Honey
A ribbon   A white tea cup

Write the bad-tempered person's name on a piece of paper. Place it at the bottom of the tea cup. Put the lodestone on top of the paper.

Cover the stone with eight slivers of poplar and eight pieces of the other ingredients. Add eight spoonfuls of honey.

Cut the ribbon the same length as the circumference of the bad-tempered person's head. Tie eight knots in it and place it on top of the cup's contents. Place the cup and its contents before Obatala for eight days.

TO ESCAPE THE LAW

Rub your head with two quail hens. Bite their heads off and let the blood drip on your head. Spread their feathers up and down the street.

TO KEEP THE POLICE AWAY

Grind sage leaves into a powder and blow on your door.

TO OBTAIN A PRISONER'S RELEASE

A rooster   Cemetery dust
Cotton thread in red, black, white, yellow, blue, green, and brown

Sacrifice the rooster to Elegua. Toast the rooster's feathers and grind them to a powder. Mix the powder with the dust.

Tear out the rooster's tongue and wind it tightly in the different colored threads. It is to be given to the prisoner to unwind in his or her cell.

Sprinkle a light, but steady, stream of powder from the Orisha's house to the jail and back again.

TO WIN A TRIAL

A black rooster   Two doves   Three pins   Honey
Balsam   Essential oils   Rue   Basil   Witch hazel
Cotton thread of the seven colors
Abre camino *(bunchosia media)*   Bran   Sunflowers

Rub the accused person's nude body with the rooster and the two doves. Sacrifice them to Elegua. Cut out the rooster's tongue and pierce it with the pins.

Rub the tongue with honey, the balsam, the oils, the rue, and the basil. Write the judge's name and the names of the accusing witnesses on a piece of paper. Wrap the anointed tongue, with the rue and the basil, in the paper. Wrap the little package tightly with the colored threads in front of your Elegua. As you wind, petition Elegua for the accused person's liberty.

After the package is wound, place it on the floor and step on it three times saying: "In the name of God and Elegua. All my enemies will be under my control, without the power to speak, accuse me, or defend themselves. Their tongues are tied with this spell."

Before the trial, the accused must bathe in a tub in which witch hazel, bran, sunflowers, and abre camino have been steeped. On the trial date, the accused will take the small package into court. He or she will place it on the courtroom floor, without anyone's seeing it, and will carefully step on it three times while repeating the above prayer.

TO STAY OUT OF JAIL

Dust from your house   Corn meal   Dust from the jail
A red ribbon   A rooster   Cotton
Red, black, and white thread   Dry wine
Florida water cologne   Orange water

Mix equal parts of the dusts with the corn meal. Place the powder on top of a yard of the ribbon and put it next to Elegua for three days.

The day before the trial, sacrifice a rooster to Elegua and tear out its tongue. Write the names of the accusing persons on a piece of paper. Wrap the tongue in cotton and then in the paper. Wind the package tightly with the thread and give it to the accused.

Offer dry wine, Florida water, and orange water to Elegua on the trial date. Cut the red ribbon in two and tie a piece to the accused's right arm and another to the left arm. Divide the powder mixture in two paper packets.

Place a packet at each of the street corners of the court building. The accused should carry the rooster's tongue package into court.

TO AVOID THE POLICE

Dust   Two vultures   A rooster   A guinea hen
A white cloth   A red cloth   A leather bag
An alligator's tooth

Collect dust at noon. Sacrifice a vulture and take out its heart. Sacrifice the rooster. Soak the white cloth in its blood. Place the cloth out in the sun to dry and lay the vulture's heart on it until it dries as well.

Collect dust at midnight. Sacrifice the second vulture and take out its heart. Sacrifice the guinea hen and soak the red cloth in its blood. Put the cloth outside to dry. Lay the vulture's heart on it until it dries as well.

When the hearts are dry, grind them into a powder. Mix the powder with a pinch of the dust collected at noon and then at midnight. Put the mixture in a small leather bag with the tooth and sew the bag shut. Wear the talisman close to your body.

Talismans, Spells, and Implorations (Ebos) (cont.)

Ebos for Luck

TO HAVE GOOD FORTUNE

EVERY YEAR, FIND OUT WHAT ORISHAS RULE THE YEAR AND FLY BANners in their favorite colors from your front door and at your place of business.

TO HAVE GOOD LUCK

Spread candies and pennies in the corners of your house. Do the same at street corners and at crossroads. It will make Elegua happy, and he will favor you.

TO HAVE GOOD LUCK

Wear ornaments of coral and jet around your neck. Wearing these is especially effective for children. The ornaments should be washed in holy water and coconut water every now and then to refresh them.

TO ATTRACT LUCK

Wear an alligator's tooth around your neck. Never go near the ocean or a river with it, or it will lose its powers.

TO HAVE GOOD LUCK

A red apple   Five yellow roses   A red rose   A white rose
Seven lettuce leaves   A half quart of milk   Honey
Abre camino *(bunchosia media)*   Wild mint

Cinnamon sticks Marigolds Florida water cologne
Cologne Almond oil Patchouli oil Bath salts
A red candle

Blend the apple, the flowers, the lettuce, the milk, seven spoonfuls of honey, seven leaves of abre camino, seven mint leaves, seven cinnamon sticks, and seven marigolds until a smooth, thick liquid is obtained. Add a small bottle of Florida water, a small bottle of cologne, and seven drops of each of the essential oils.

Fill up the tub with hot water and pour in the mixture. Add the bath salts. Light the red candle and relax in the bath. Repeat the procedure seven days in a row.

TO HAVE GOOD LUCK

Macerate a handful of laurel leaves in water and add to a hot bath.

TO HAVE GOOD LUCK

Cover a white bed sheet in laurel leaves. Sleep on them.

FOR GOOD LUCK

Pine needles Lavender leaves Laurel leaves
Geranium leaves Patchouli

Take out the stuffing from your pillow. Mix equal portions of the pine needles and the different leaves until you have the same volume of material as the stuffing you took out. Sprinkle with a couple of drops of patchouli and stuff your pillow with the herbal mixture. Sleep with it every night.

TO HAVE GOOD LUCK

Parsley Boneset Jamaican rosewood Five yellow roses
Honey Cologne Powdered eggshell A yellow candle

Crush the herbs in water. Add five spoonfuls of honey and a small bottle of the cologne. Place the mixture in an open container and leave out exposed to the sun a day and exposed a night to the dew.

Divide the mixture into five equal parts. To each, add a whole rose.

For five consecutive days, light the candle after your bath or shower and, without toweling yourself dry, splash on the mixture. Let it dry on your body.

Ebos for Money

TO BRING PROSPERITY

Orange rind   Dried orange leaves
Brown sugar   An iron pot

Place the ingredients in the pot and burn them. Smother the fire and leave the smoldering mixture smoking heavily. Offer the incense to Oshun: *"oshun oguao mi inle oshun igua iya mio igua iko bo si iya mi guasi iya mi omo y alorde oguo mi inle ashe oshun."* Or, respectfully pray to Oshun in your own language for the money and economic prosperity that you need.

TO ATTRACT MONEY

A multicolored bowl   A multicolored cloak
Nine old pennies   Alum   Oil   Red ocher
Dust from consecrated ground   Rain water

Place the pennies in the bowl. Cover them with nine pieces of alum, nine spoonfuls of oil, nine pinches of red ocher and of the dust. Add enough rain water to cover the ingredients.

Cover the bowl with the multicolored cloak and place before Oya. When the money comes, part must be used to buy a sacrifice to Oya.

TO MAKE A MAN GIVE MONEY TO A WOMAN

A coin   Oil   Red ocher
White, blue, red, yellow, black, green, and brown thread

Obtain a coin from the man. Wrap it in the different colors of thread until no part of the coin can be seen. Place the wrapped coin in a dish full of oil and seven pinches of red ocher. Let it soak for seven days. Keep the coin in a safe place and never spend it.

TO ATTRACT MONEY

A lodestone   Rue   Rosemary   Anise
Sweet basil   A silver coin   Holy water
Red and black thread   A red cloth
A black cloth

Place a lodestone in a deep dish. Cross a sprig of rue with a sprig of rosemary on top of the stone. Cross a line of anise with a sprig of sweet basil on top of the first cross.

Wind black thread around the coin. Wind crosswise with red thread. Lay the coin on top of the herbal crosses. Sprinkle three times with holy water. Say three Hail Marys. Cover the dish with the cloths and leave before your Elegua for three days. Always carry the coin with you.

TO GET MONEY FROM A RICH FRIEND

A coconut shell   Oil   Red wine   Nine pennies

Write your friend's name on a piece of paper and place it in the coconut shell. Put the pennies on top. Add nine spoonfuls of red wine. Fill the shell the rest of the way with oil. Insert a wick.

Burn the lamp in your yard for nine days. Then, go talk to your friend about money.

TO MAKE A DEBTOR PAY

Three needles   Honey   Rose honey   A candle

Write the name of the debtor on a piece of paper. Pierce the paper with the needles. Place it in a glass containing equal parts of the two honeys. Place the glass before your Elegua.

Light the candle and place it next to the glass. Petition Elegua for your money. If you receive it, you must make a sacrifice to him.

TO GET AN INHERITANCE

An eggshell   Rain water   Parsley
Watercress   Rose honey

Write the names of the interested parties and the name of the lawyer on a piece of paper. Place the paper in a deep dish. Soften the eggshell in the rain water and cover the paper with the paste.

Finely chop parsley and watercress and mix equal parts together. Cover the eggshell paste with the chopped herbs. Pour rose honey over the whole thing. Place the dish on a high shelf in your house until the matter is resolved.

TO ATTRACT MONEY

Tobacco flowers	Honey	Pompeii perfume
1800 cologne	Mint oil	White roses

Pour the two bottles of perfume into a large bottle. Add seven tobacco flowers and seven roses. Pour in seven spoonfuls of honey and seven drops of mint oil.

Pour some of the mixture in your bath every day for seven days. If your luck is very bad, do it for twenty-one days.

TO ATTRACT MONEY

Three yellow roses	The milk from three coconuts
Florida water cologne	Coconut meat Dry wine
Cinnamon sticks	Sweet basil Pumpkin rind

Fill a large container with the roses, the coconut milk, a large bottle of Florida water, three small pieces of coconut meat, a glass of dry wine, three cinnamon sticks, three large handfuls of sweet basil, and five pieces of pumpkin rind. Add about five gallons of water.

Bathe with the mixture for three days in a row. Skip three days and then bathe with it for five days in a row.

TO ATTRACT MONEY

Balsam apples	Peppergrass	Honey	River water
Pompeii cologne	White roses	Yellow roses	
Red roses	Holy water		

In a large container, put five balsam apples, five sprigs of peppergrass, five spoonfuls of honey, five of each color of rose, and five drops of holy water. Add about five gallons of clean river water and the bottle of cologne. Let the mixture sit for a day. Bathe with the mixture.

TO ATTRACT MONEY

Cow's milk   Goat's milk   Coconut milk   Holy water

Mix the liquids in equal parts. Bathe yourself in the morning, before sunrise.

TO ATTRACT MONEY

Dress in yellow and go to the ocean or to a river. Walk into the water, while dressed, with a bottle of honey. Rub your whole body with the honey, especially your head. Let the water wash it off. Don't swim.

TO ATTRACT MONEY

Wild flowers   Coconut oil   Coconut soap
Green tobacco leaves   Rosemary   Wild mint
Maiden's hair fern   Myrrh   Pompeii cologne

Gather three handfuls of wild flowers along three different paths. Put them in a large container. Add three spoonfuls of coconut oil and three bars of coconut soap, three tobacco leaves, three sprigs of rosemary and three of wild mint, and three sprigs of maiden's hair fern. Add three drops of myrrh and a bottle of the cologne. Pour in about five gallons of water.

Bathe on three Mondays in a row. After each bath, give Elegua a little bit of his favorite food.

TO ATTRACT MONEY

Rose petals   Gladioli   White lilies   Jasmine
Marigold   Sunflowers   Pompeii cologne
Guerlain cologne   Sol de Oro cologne
Florida water cologne   River water   Coconut water

Place seven rose petals in a large container. Add seven of each of the flowers, a small bottle of each cologne, and the water from five coconuts. Add about five gallons of river water. Bathe with the mixture before sunrise for seven days in a row.

Ebos for Work

TO GET A BETTER JOB

Five diamond chips   A chicken

When you want to get a better job or improve your work situation in any way, take the five diamond chips (or one if it's all your budget allows) and place them in Oshun's tureen. Sacrifice the chicken and allow the blood to drip over the diamond chips while you Moyuba Oshun.

Perform this Ebo on a Saturday or on the fifth day of the month. If you don't have a tureen, petition Oshun at a river's edge.

TO OBTAIN A JOB

Rub your hands with corojo oil and honey. Lick your hands three times and ask for the job.

TO GET A RAISE AT WORK

Star anise   Alum   Peanuts

Grind each of the ingredients into a powder. Blend equal parts together and sprinkle the mixture around your work place.

Ebos to Purify Your House or Business

TO PURIFY YOUR HOUSE AFTER MOVING IN

Dried sweet basil   Dried eucalyptus leaves   Myrrh

If you have just moved into a house and feel strange vibrations or entities, prepare a large quantity of equal parts of basil and eucalyptus. Add a little of the myrrh.

Fill a large fireproof container such as an iron pot with the mixture. Set fire to the leaves, smother the fire, and walk the smoking mixture all over the house.

Close all doors and windows, place the smoldering iron pot on a fireproof surface (such as pieces of metal or tile), and leave the house for four to five hours. When you return and air out the house, all strange influences will be gone.

TO REMOVE A CURSE AGAINST YOUR HOUSE OR BUSINESS

Banana leaves   Six Espanta Muerto sticks
A stick from the rose apple   Corojo butter
Rope from agave fibers   Dry eucalyptus leaves

Smear the banana leaves and the sticks with lots of corojo butter. Wrap the sticks in the banana leaves and tie the bundle together with the agave cord.

Place the eucalyptus leaves in a plate and burn them until they smolder and produce a lot of smoke. Take the smoking leaves all through your house or place of business, making sure that the smoke gets in all the corners. Stop at each door and ask that the curse be lifted from you.

When you have thoroughly fumigated your house or place of business, leave the eucalyptus ashes and the banana leaf bundle at the door of the person who cursed you (if you know who it is). If you don't know who cursed you, spread a bed sheet on the street and leave the ashes and the package on it. Return home and give yourself an herbal bath to drive away any traces of the spirits of the dead.

TO REMOVE EVIL INFLUENCES FROM YOUR HOUSE

A coconut   Powdered eggshell

Whiten the coconut with the powdered eggshell. Go to the room farthest from the front door. Place the coconut on the floor and kick it from room to room until you reach the front door. Give the coconut a good kick out the front door. Perform this Ebo whenever your house feels "uneasy."

TO PROTECT A NEW HOUSE

Four silver nails three to four inches long
Twenty-one herbs belonging to twelve major Orishas
A duck   A dove   A rooster   A chicken

A guinea hen (All animals are to be white.)

Have a jeweler make up the nails. Prepare an Omiero with the twenty-one herbs and the blood from all the animals.

Soak the silver nails in the Omiero for twenty-four hours. The following day, at sunrise, bury one of the nails at each of the four corners of the house, touching the walls.

TO REMOVE NEGATIVE INFLUENCES FROM A HOUSE

Paint a live turtle blue. Allow it to walk around the house for seven days. Let it wander around the yard as well, but don't let it get lost.

At the end of the seven days, take the turtle to the water and let it go. Offer a watermelon to Yemaya.

TO KEEP YOUR HOUSE FREE OF SPIRITS

Don't rock empty rocking chairs.

TO KEEP ENEMIES AND RIVALS AWAY FROM YOUR HOUSE

Boneset root	Rusted iron	Arsenic	Sulphur
Red ocher	Ground deer antler	Rock salt	Balsam
A scorpion	Cooking oil		

Fry the scorpion in the oil until the scorpion is dissolved. Save the oil.

Write the person's name on a piece of paper. Place the paper at the bottom of a clay pot and burn it to ashes. Put the boneset on top of the ashes. Add three slivers of rusted iron. Cover all with the powders. Add three grains of the rock salt and the balsam. Cover all the ingredients in the oil. Insert a wick.

Place the lamp in front of Elegua and light it. Leave it lit for three days. While the lamp is lit, pray that Elegua drive your enemies away. Throw water out the front door three times after each prayer.

TO MAKE A NEIGHBOR MOVE

A wasp's nest	Coal	Guinea pepper	Rock salt
An egg	Red ocher		

Powder a piece of wasp's nest, coal, and four grains of guinea pepper.

Add three grains of rock salt. Mix equal parts of the powder. Let the egg soak in oil and red ocher for three days and nights. Throw the egg at your neighbor's door and blow the powder after it so that it sticks to the remnants of the egg.

TO MAKE A NEIGHBOR MOVE

Powdered eggshell   An egg from a black chicken
Nightshade

Dry and powder the egg. Dry and powder the nightshade. Mix with equal parts of powdered eggshell. Blow this powder inside your neighbor's house.

TO MAKE A NEIGHBOR MOVE

The white of an egg   Seven needles   Cowhage
Iron filings   Peppercorns
Dust from the four corners of a crossroads
A feather from a guinea hen

Pierce the egg and blow the white out. Stick the needles into the egg. Burn the feather and reduce it to ashes. Grind the rest of the ingredients into a powder and mix in equal parts.

Throw the egg at your neighbor's door. Blow the powder after it.

TO PREVENT THE RENTAL OF A HOUSE

Carbon dust   Rock dust   Benzoin resin

Grind the ingredients into a powder and mix in equal parts. Sprinkle the mixture inside the house.

TO HAVE YOUR LAWYER WIN A PROPERTY SUIT

A peacock feather   A guinea hen feather
Earth from the four corners of the property

Toast the feathers and grind them to a powder. Mix in equal quantities with the earth. Sift the mixture to a very fine powder. The lawyer is to sprinkle the dust on the floor of the courtroom where the case is being heard.

TO PROTECT YOUR HOUSE

Anamu (*petiveria alliacea:* garlic herb native to Cuba)
Three large iron nails   Red, white, and black thread
Wax   Powdered eggshell   An egg   Water   Wine
Cut the thread into seven-inch sections. Twist three of the white threads, two of the black threads, and two of the red threads together. Rub with wax to make a stiff twine. Make three pieces of the twine.

Put the nails in a fire until they are red hot. While they are still hot, wrap each nail in anamu leaves and wind tight with the twine.

Cover the egg in the powdered eggshell. Make a triangle with the nails. Stand up the egg in the triangle. Sprinkle the amulet with water and wine every day.

Ebos for Love

TO WIN A WOMAN

Coral   Cinnamon   Creme de Menthe   Anise
Powder the ingredients and mix them with a few drops of the Creme de Menthe. When drunk or eaten, the mixture will turn the most indifferent woman into a passionate lover.

TO CONQUER A LOVER

Chew a small stick of Jamaica rosewood and either chew it or leave it inside your mouth while you speak to the person you are trying to seduce. This works equally well in a business meeting.

TO RESOLVE ROMANTIC PROBLEMS

Parsley   Honey   Cinnamon sticks   Dry corn
Mix all the ingredients together, reserving a sprig of parsley. Place the mixture in a high place in your house. Every time you speak with the one you love, you must have the sprig of parsley with you.

TO WIN A LOVER

Write the person's name with India ink on a small piece of papyrus. Put the slip of paper under a gourd filled with an Omiero made with seven herbs belonging to Yemaya and Oshun.

TO AROUSE VIRILITY IN MEN AND PASSION IN WOMEN

Sea turtle eggs　　Honey　　Cinnamon sticks

Dry the eggs and powder them. Brew cinnamon tea, stir in the powdered eggs, and sweeten the mixture with honey. Drink three times a day.

TO ATTRACT A LOVER

Sea water　　Indigo dye　　Sugar cane syrup
Corojo butter　　Pork lard　　Vegetable oil　　Mercury
Cocoa butter　　A cotton wick　　Seven pins　　Blue thread

Write the lover's name at the bottom of a large pot. Fill the pot with the oil. Add small quantities of the rest of the ingredients. Insert the wick.

Go to the seashore. Tie the seven pins together with the thread. Hold them up before you and walk out to the surf, calling out your lover's name seven times. Light the lamp.

Take the burning lamp back home and allow it to burn for seven days. At the end of seven days, take the lamp back out to the seashore and let the waves sweep it away. Petition Yemaya to have your lover at your feet.

TO ATTRACT A LOVER

Dirt from a hillside　　Mercury　　Red wine　　Sulphur
Red ocher　　Borax　　Two slugs　　Two doves
An arrow made of white metal　　Almond oil

Paint a white stripe around a new clay pot. Write the name of the person you desire on a piece of paper and place it in the pot. Cover the paper with a handful of dirt. Add the mercury, a little red wine, a pinch of the powders, and the slugs.

Sacrifice the two doves to Obatala. Cut out their hearts and pin them together with the metal arrow. Add the hearts to the pot. Fill with almond oil.

Insert the cotton wick, light it, and allow the lamp to burn for sixteen days. After sixteen days, bury the pot and its contents at the foot of a kapok tree. Dress in white for another sixteen days.

TO ATTRACT A LOVER

Red ocher   Sulphur   Borax   Powdered poplar leaves
Three pins   Cooking oil

Write the loved one's name on a piece of paper four times and pierce the paper with the pins. Place the paper inside a large colorful teapot. Add a pinch of the four powders and the oil. Insert a wick and burn the lamp for nine days.

TO ATTRACT A LOVER

A red apple   Corojo oil   Six okras
Corn meal   Mercury

Place the apple in a gourd. Cover it with the oil. Add a small amount of the other ingredients. Insert a cotton wick and light the lamp before Chango's tureen.

TO SEDUCE A MAN

Cooking oil   Red wine   Aguardiente   Seven needles
Black thread   White thread

Pour the cooking oil, a cup of red wine, and a cup of aguardiente in a new pot. Write the man's name on a piece of paper and pierce it with the seven needles. Roll the paper up into a cylinder and wind the black and white thread around it. Float the paper on the oil. Insert a wick.

Light the lamp and burn it for nine days. At the end of the ninth day, take out the needles and bury them.

TO ATTRACT A LOVER

A dove   Seven pins   Sesame oil   Olive oil
Almond oil   Honey   Red ocher

Cut out the dove's heart. Write the person's name on a piece of paper and wrap the heart in it. Pierce the packet with the seven pins and place inside a pot.

Pour in equal parts of the oils. Add a pinch of the powder and a spoonful of honey. Insert a wick.

Light the lamp and allow it to burn for five days. On the fifth day, bury the pot and go visit the desired person.

TO ATTRACT AND DOMINATE A LOVER

Cooking oil   Black ink   Mercury   Seven peppercorns
A length of narrow ribbon

Pour the cooking oil into a pot. Add a few drops of ink, mercury, and the peppercorns.

Remove all your clothes and stand before your Elegua. Tie the piece of ribbon around your waist. While tying seven knots in the ribbon say: "By the seven words that Christ said on the cross. With two, I look at you. With three, I see you. With the Father, the Son, and the Holy Ghost, let [name] come and be at my feet."

TO ATTRACT A LOVER

A dove   Four pins   A round river pebble   Olive oil
Red ocher   Rock candy   Sesame oil

Place the pebble in a pot. Sacrifice the dove and let the blood drip on the pebble. Cut the heart out of the dove and pierce it with the four pins. Place the heart in the pot along with the rest of the ingredients and cover with the oils. Insert a wick and light. When the lamp goes out, remove the pebble and wear it as a talisman.

TO ATTRACT A LOVER

Whale oil   Almond oil   Corojo oil   Balsam oil
Mercury   Water

Mix the oils together in a small container. Add a drop of mercury and a spoonful of water. Write the lover's name on a piece of paper and put it in the oil. Insert a wick and burn the lamp.

TO ATTRACT A LOVER

A glass of water   Honey   Camphor   Poppies
Mercury   A candle

At noon, write the loved one's name on a piece of paper and place it in the glass of water. Add a small quantity of the other ingredients. Light a candle next to the glass.

TO SEDUCE A LOVER

A large new tea cup   A lodestone   Five needles
A dove   Five varieties of sweet wine   Olive oil   Honey
Mercury   Five cotton wicks

Write the name of the person you love on a piece of paper. Pierce the paper with the needles. Place the paper at the bottom of the cup and weigh it down with the lodestone. Sacrifice the dove over the cup and allow the blood to pour over the stone. Add a spoonful of each of the wines, five drops of mercury, and five spoonfuls of honey. Fill the rest of the cup with olive oil. Insert the wicks. Light and burn for five days.

TO SEDUCE A MAN

Seven earthworms   Menstrual blood   Excrement
Hair   Genital hair

Collect seven earthworms. Lay them in the sun to dry. Also collect a little of your menstrual blood, a pinch of your excrement, hairs from your head, and hair from your genitals. Lay them on a plate and let them dry in the sun.

When all the ingredients are thoroughly dry, grind them to a very fine powder. Administer the powder in the man's food or drink.

TO SEDUCE A MAN

Menstrual blood   Nail trimmings   Hair   Genital hair
Armpit hair   Poppy seeds   Root of rue   Amansa guapo
A hummingbird heart

Collect a bit of your menstrual blood, nail trimmings from each of your fingers, and hair from your head, armpits, and genitals.

Lay all the ingredients on a plate and add the hummingbird heart, three poppy seeds, the root, and the amansa guapo. Set everything in the sun to dry.

When everything is thoroughly dry, grind it to a very fine powder. Put the powder next to your Elegua for three days. Administer the powder in the man's food or drink.

If a man wants to prepare this powder to seduce a woman, replace the menstrual blood with semen.

TO SEDUCE A MAN OR A WOMAN

Cooking oil   Urine   Red wine   Lemon juice
Rock candy   Mercury   A black dove   Seven needles
Hair   Seven earthworms   Menstrual blood

In a clay pot, place seven drops of your urine, seven spoonfuls of red wine, seven spoonfuls of lemon juice, seven pieces of candy, and seven drops of mercury. Sacrifice the dove over the pot and stir in the blood. Fill the rest of the pot with the oil.

Write the person's name backwards on a piece of paper. Wrap the dove's heart in the paper and pierce it with the seven needles. Place it in the clay pot. Insert a wick and burn the lamp for seven days.

While the lamp burns, dry the earthworms, the blood, and the hair in the sun. On the seventh day, unwrap the heart and toast it. Reduce it, the worms, the blood, and the hair to a powder. Administer in the food or drink.

A man needs to replace the menstrual blood with semen.

TO BE SEDUCTIVE

Talisman (perfumed body powder)
Five hairs from a stray bitch
Powdered eggshell from an infertile dove egg
Ground antler   Incense   Borax   Valerian powder
Cinnamon powder   Five pieces of coral

Grind the five corals and the five hairs from a stray bitch into a fine powder. Mix with the body powder. Add five pinches of the powdered eggshell, the antler, the incense, the borax, the valerian, and the cinnamon. After the powder has been thoroughly mixed, sprinkle on your body.

TO ATTRACT A LOVER

Pompeii face powder   Cinnamon   Valerian powder
Holy water   Mercury

Add a pinch of the other powders to the face powder. Make a cross on the surface of the mix with the holy water. Add a drop of mercury.

TO MARRY THE PERSON YOU WANT

Rub your hands with powdered eggshell before you shake hands with him or her.

Ebos to Insure Faithfulness

TO STOP A HUSBAND FROM BEING UNFAITHFUL

Yellow cloth   Dried corn   Honey
Cinnamon sticks   Cinnamon oil   Cotton
Two lodestones   A candle

When you know that your husband is unfaithful, take a little cutting of his hair and a few of his nail parings. Place them and all the ingredients, except the candle and the cinnamon oil, in the yellow cloth and make a tight bundle. Sprinkle the bundle with cinnamon oil and burn the candle to Oshun daily for five days.

If the unfaithful husband has actually left the house, add the blood of a chicken to Oshun's tureen before making this Ebo.

TO KEEP A SPOUSE FROM RUNNING OFF

A clay pot   Yellow paint   Corn meal
Cinnamon powder   Cinnamon sticks   A powdered lodestone
Two lodestones   Iron filings   Five cowrie shells
Five white chickens   A candle   Coconut oil

Cinnamon oil

Paint the clay pot yellow. Fill the pot with corn meal, powdered and stick cinnamon, powdered lodestone, the filings, the whole lodestones, and the five cowrie shells.

Sacrifice the five chickens and allow the blood to soak into the corn meal. Pluck the chickens and fill the pot to the top with feathers.

Keep the pot hidden from your spouse. Light a candle to the pot at sunset for five consecutive days and sprinkle it with a few drops of coconut and cinnamon oils. Dispose of the Ebo in a river.

TO HOLD ON TO A WANDERING HUSBAND

Almond oil   Honey   Holy water   Egg yolk
Yellow cloth   Red ribbon

Fill a gourd with almond oil. Add small quantities of honey, holy water, and egg yolk. Insert a wick.

Light the lamp as you petition Oshun. Wrap the yellow cloth around your middle and tie it tight with the red ribbon. Wear the girdle for five days.

TO HAVE A LOVER RETURN

A large gourd   Two chicken feet   An egg   Linseed oil
Florida water cologne   Marjoram   Paprika
A piece of your lover's clothing or jewelry   A cotton wick

Write your lover's name on a piece of paper. Place the gourd on top of the paper. Put five chicken nails, the egg, Florida water, a little paprika, marjoram, and a strip of the clothing or the piece of jewelry in the gourd. Fill it up with the linseed oil and insert the wick.

Petition Oshun for your lover's return as you light the lamp. Allow it to burn for five days. Dispose of it in a river.

TO TIE A LOVER TO YOU

Obtain seven ribbons in the colors of the Seven African Powers (white, blue, red, yellow, black, green, and brown). Weave them together in a cord.

Smear the completed cord with plenty of corojo butter and a little bit of coconut oil. Make seven knots along the length of the cord and place it in front of a photo or the name of the person you want to tie to you. Burn a candle before the cord for seven days.

TO TIE A LOVER TO YOU

Olive oil	Mercury	Sulphur	Sweet wine
Aguardiente	Five small dolls	Yellow thread	

Buy a metal pot and fill it with olive oil. Add small quantities of the mercury and sulphur. Pour in five spoonfuls of wine and aguardiente. Make up the dolls to look like the person you want to tie to you. Tie them together with yellow thread and float them in the oil. Place a cotton wick in the oil.

Petition Oshun as you light the wick. Burn the lamp for five days and dispose of it in a river.

TO TIE A LOVER TO YOU

Cooking oil	Honey	Brown sugar	Rock candy
Five pins	Five needles	Five cotton wicks	

Write your lover's name on a piece of paper. Pierce the paper with the pins and needles and place it at the bottom of a large tea cup. Cover the paper completely with small amounts of the honey, sugar, and candy. Fill the cup the rest of the way with the oil. Insert the five wicks. Light the lamp and allow it to burn for five days.

TO TIE A LOVER TO YOU

Elegua's herbs	Smoked fish	Smoked jutia	Holy water
Red ocher	Sulphur	Borax	Balsam
Valerian powder	Powdered poppy seeds	Powdered rue root	
Two small dolls	Small wooden chains	A lodestone	
Three iron nails	Sesame oil	Balsam oil	Patchouli oil
Poppy oil	Honey	Aguardiente	Cotton
White thread	Black thread	A wooden box	

Prepare an Omiero with Elegua's herbs. Write your lover's name on a piece of paper and wrap the paper in cotton. If the person to be tied is a man, add a little of his semen; if a woman, a few drops of her menstrual blood. Place the paper wrapped in cotton between the two dolls. Tie the two dolls together with the wooden chains.

Sprinkle the dolls with the essential oils, aguardiente, and honey. Begin winding them with the thread. As you wind, insert the nails into the mummy as well as into the lodestone. Continue winding with thread and intermingling the rest of the ingredients until the dolls are completely hidden.

Soak the doll mummy in the Omiero as you petition Elegua to make your relationship as tight as that of the dolls. Leave the bundle soaking in the Omiero for three days. After the three days, place the wrapped dolls in the box, nail it shut, and bury it at the base of a kapok tree or a palm tree.

TO TIE A LOVER TO YOU

Pins   Corn silk   Thread

Take the inner soles out of your lover's shoes. Also obtain a little bit of the person's hair and clothing.

Write your name on a piece of paper. Write your lover's name on another piece of paper. Lay the papers over one another so that they form a cross. Pin them together and wrap them in corn silk.

Sandwich the papers and the rest of the items in between the inner soles. Wrap everything tightly with the thread and bury the package.

TO TIE A WOMAN TO YOU

Sugar cane   Corn starch   Taro
Immature corn   A fox's tail   Ginger
Five pieces of coral   A ball of cotton
Pubic hairs taken while she is menstruating

Tie all the ingredients into a bundle and bury it.

TO KEEP A MAN FAITHFUL

Five coral crosses   A piece of amber   Honey   Ferns
A coin   Indian lotus (nelumbo)

In a jar before Oshun's tureen, place twenty-five drops of honey. One by one, grind the coral and the amber to a fine powder. Do a Moyuba for Oshun as you add the powder to the honey. Take the jar to a river and pray to Oshun.

Take a large leaf of Indian lotus. Leave a coin for Osain in exchange. Place the leaf in the jar and wrap the jar in the ferns.

After five days, unwrap the jar. Press out the juice from the leaf and wash your genitals with the juice. Moisten a piece of cotton with the honey mixture and insert it in your vagina. Take the cotton back out and make love with the man you want to tie.

TO TIE A LOVER TO YOU

A male and a female lizard
Black, white, and red thread
Seven needles   Aguardiente

Tie the lizards together with the three colors of thread. Pierce the lizards with the needles and pack them in mud taken from your lover's shoes.

Obtain a piece of your lover's sweaty clothing. Soak it in aguardiente. Wrap the mud ball in the piece of clothing and place it before your Elegua. Petition Elegua so that he will help you hold on to your lover.

TO TIE A MAN TO A WOMAN

A white handkerchief   Aguardiente   Three basil roots

Gather some of the man's semen and place it on a white handkerchief. Let it dry. When the semen is dry, tear the handkerchief into fourteen strips. Tie a knot in each strip. Tie all the knotted strips end to end and place them under your Elegua along with the roots and a glass of aguardiente.

TO TIE A LOVER TO YOU

Write your lover's first name on a piece of paper. Turn the paper ninety degrees and write the last name so that it crosses the first name. Place a pair of scissors on top of the piece of paper.

TO TIE A LOVER TO YOU

Salt Saffron Anise Cumin Seven pebbles
Three dried twigs A hermit crab Two bags Dry wine

Dampen the salt, anise, saffron, and cumin and mix into a stiff paste. Make five figurines (either male or female).

Gather seven pebbles from the four corners of the block where your lover lives. While gathering the pebbles, also gather the twigs. Go to the seashore and capture a hermit crab. Sweep up a little dust from your lover's footprints. Write his or her name on a piece of paper.

Put the figurines and all the other items in a bag. Sew it up and place it inside a second bag. Sprinkle the package with dry wine and leave it at a street corner.

TO TIE A LOVER TO YOU

Swallow a grain of corn whole, without chewing it. Pick it out of your excrement once it passes through you. Add the grain of corn to the food of the person you want to tie to you.

TO KEEP A LOVER FROM LEAVING TOWN

A glass Coffee grounds Water
A candle Corojo butter

Write your lover's first and last names backwards in the form of a cross on a piece of paper. Place the paper in the bottom of a glass. Cover the paper with coffee grounds and fill the rest of the glass with water. Place the glass next to your Elegua.

Cover the candle with corojo butter. Place it next to the glass. As you light it, petition Elegua to prevent your lover from leaving.

TO MAKE YOUR LOVER COME BACK TO TOWN

Cut out a paper silhouette the same size as your lover. Write your lover's name upon it seven times. Cut the names out of the paper figurine with new scissors. Place the strips of paper at the foot of your Elegua. Leave them there for seven days.

On the seventh day, burn the silhouette and the strips of paper with your lover's name. Toss the ashes in the direction where your lover is.

TO MAKE YOUR LOVER COME BACK TO TOWN

A new deep white plate   Almond oil   Coconut oil
Three cotton wicks

Write your lover's name on a piece of paper and lay it inside the plate. Fill the plate with equal parts of the oils. Insert the wicks. Light and let the lamp burn for three days.

TO MAKE YOUR LOVER COME BACK TO TOWN

A lodestone   Three needles   Sweet wine   Mercury
Red ocher   A glass of water

Write your lover's name on a piece of paper. Write your name so that it makes a cross over it. Pierce the paper with the needles, and place it at the bottom of a small clay pot. Weigh it down with the lodestone. Add three pinches of red ocher, three spoonfuls of wine, and a small dollop of mercury. Put a glass of water next to the pot.

TO TIE A LOVER TO YOU

A lodestone   Dry wine
Three horseshoe nails   An egg
Parsley   Amansa guapo   A candle

Obtain your lover's wash cloth. Write your lover's name on a piece of paper and place it on the cloth.

Wash a lodestone in dry wine and put it on top of the paper. Place the rest of the ingredients on the paper. Wrap the cloth around everything and make a tight bundle. Sprinkle the package every Friday with dry wine and light a candle next to it.

TO TIE A LOVER TO YOU

A nail   Aguardiente

Heat the nail until it is red hot and plunge it into aguardiente. Let it soak for seven days. On the seventh day, reheat the nail and sprinkle it with aguardiente. Drive the nail into a beam or wall in your house while calling out your lover's name.

TO TIE A LOVER TO YOU

A lodestone	Sea water	A rooster	Red ocher
Sulphur	Borax	Mercury	Seven pieces of poplar root
Watercress juice	Sweet wine	Cooking oil	A cotton wick

Write your lover's name on a piece of paper. Place it at the bottom of a deep pot. Weigh it down with the lodestone. Sacrifice the rooster over the pot and let all the blood drain over the paper and the lodestone.

Add seven pinches of the three powders, seven drops of mercury, the seven roots, and seven spoonfuls of the juice and of the sweet wine. Pour in seven cups of sea water and fill to the top with cooking oil. Insert a wick and burn for seven days.

Where to Obtain the Ingredients

If you live in a large city with a pronounced Latin population, you should have no trouble. Look in your Yellow Pages under "Religious Articles and Supplies." Any business with a name like "Elegua's" or "Botanica" will be able to provide anything you need. Many of the Ebos described in this book are available pre-mixed and packaged, as aerosol sprays and as Ebo "kits."

To obtain animals for sacrifices, look in the Yellow Pages under "Pet Stores." Look for those stores in the same neighborhoods as the "Botanicas."

REFERENCES

Aguabella, Francisco. *Santeria Oro Cantado con Tambores Bata.* 3 cassettes.

El Arte de Tirar los Caracoles e Interpretar los Cocos (Los Oraculos de Biague y Dialoggun). Miami: Language Research Press, 1958.

Cabrera, Lydia. *Koeko Iyawo: Aprende Novicia (Pequeño Tratado de Regla Lucumi).* Miami: Ultra Graphic Corp., 1980.

_____. *El Monte (Igbo. Finda. Ewe Orisha. Vititi Nfinda).* 6th ed. Miami: Daytona Printing Corp., 1986.

_____. *La Regla Kimbisa del Santo Cristo del Buen Viaje.* 2d ed. Miami: Ediciones Universal, 1986.

_____. *Reglas de Congo (Palo Monte Mayombe).* 2d ed. Miami: Ediciones Universal, 1986.

Consejos y Recetas Espirituales.

Cortez, Julio Garcia. *El Santo (La Ocha).* 3d ed. Miami: Ediciones Universal, 1983.

Despojos, Baños, Limpiezas, Riegos y Hechizos.

Diccionario del ñañigo y el Lucumi.

Efunde, Agun. *Los Secretos de la Santeria.* Miami: Ediciones Cubamerica, 1983.

Gaycedo, German Castro. *Mi Alma se la Dejo al Diablo.* 6th ed. Editores Colombia Ltda., 1982.

Pichardo, Ernesto. *Oduduwa Obatala.* Miami: Rex Press, Inc., 1984.

El Supremo Libro de las Velas.

Cultural Interiority

Spirits of the Night: The Vaudun Gods of Haiti
SELDEN RODMAN AND CAROLE CLEAVER

This book is a comprehensive study of a living polytheistic culture and religion. Filled with the authors' over fifty years of experience in Haiti, it debunks many of the clichés about "voodoo" (i.e., dolls attacked by pins) and reveals the joy inherent in transcendent "vaudun." Includes a bibliography and twenty black and white illustrations. (145 pp.)

The Japanese Psyche: Major Motifs in the Fairy Tales of Japan
HAYAO KAWAI

Why do so few Japanese fairy tales end in a happily-ever-after marriage? Why does the female best express the culture's ego? Kawai compares Japanese and Western tales, elucidating the former's peculiar figures and themes. Terrible women who eat people, obscene escapes from male demons, brother–sister bonds: with these elements Kawai presents the many-layered Japanese psyche. (234 pp.)

Broodmales
NOR HALL, WARREN R. DAWSON

Men becoming women? In the folk customs of couvade, a man takes on the events of a woman's body—pregnancy, labor, nursing—so that her experience becomes his. Rather bizarre than perverse or deluded, these behaviors reveal a natural symbolic process, which Hall's essay explains psychologically. Dawson's classic crosscultural study gathers evidence for what often still occurs today in men's private experiences. (173 pp.)

The Book of Life
MARSILIO FICINO—CHARLES BOER, TR.

In this fluent translation—the first in English—this underground classic of the Italian Renaissance is a guide to food, drink, sleep, mood, sexuality, song, and countless herbal and vegetable concoctions for maintaining the right balance of soul, body, and spirit. Translator's introduction (with bibliography), index. (xx, 217 pp.)

SPRING PUBLICATIONS   POB 222069   DALLAS, TX 75222
214/943-4093   FAX 943-4520